America's First Movie Theater: Louisiana's Vitascope Hall

By
Ed and Susan Poole

Learn About Network, L.L.C

America's First Movie Theater:
Louisiana's Vitascope Hall

© 2016 by Ed and Susan Poole

PUBLISHED BY:

Learn About Network, L.L.C.
P. O. Box 3181
Harvey, LA 70059
(504) 298-5267

First edition published 2016

ISBN: 978-0-9965015-1-4

IMAGES

All images featured in this book are from the private collection of the authors.

RIGHTS

All Rights Reserved. No part of this publication may be reproduced, stored in a database, or transmitted in any form, or by any means, electronic, mechanical, photocopying, recording, or otherwise, without prior written permission of the Authors/Publishers.

LIMIT OF LIABILITY/DISCLAIMER OF WARRANTY

The Authors/Publishers have used their best efforts in preparing this publication. Authors/Publishers make no representation or warranties with respect to the accuracy or completeness of the contents of this publication and specifically disclaim any implied warranties of merchantability or fitness for any particular purpose and shall in no event be liable for any loss of profit or any other commercial damage, including but not limited to special, incidental, consequential, or other damages.

ADDITIONAL COPIES

Additional copies of this publication may be ordered through HollywoodOnTheBayou.com.

TABLE OF CONTENTS

Foreword by LindaThurman ……………………...iii

About the Cover ……………………………………..v

About the Authors ……………………………………vii

Introduction ………………………………………..1

Pre-Cinema Developments ……………………….3

    Cave Drawings …………………………...3

    Magic Lantern ……………………………..5

    Photography ……………………………….7

    Optical Toys ……………………………...9

Cinema Pioneers ………………………………...15

    Eadweard Muybridge …………………..16

    Charles Emile Reynaud ………………….19

    Etienne-Jules Marey …………………...23

    Louis Aime Augustin Le Prince …………..24

    Thomas Edison and William Kennedy Laurie Dickson …………………………….29

    Auguste and Louis Lumiere ……………..34

Rise of the American Cinema 36

    Phantoscope 42

    Vitascope 54

Rock & Wainwright Purchase La Rights 61

    Spanish Fort 69

    Milneburg 71

    West End Park 74

Moving Pictures Make Their Louisiana Debut ..81

First Movie Theater in American Opens
Its Doors 93

    Canal Street 94

    Vitascope Finds a Home and Makes
    Movie History 97

    Rock and Wainwright Return to
    New Orleans the Next Season 104

Epilogue 105

References 113

Index 115

Foreword
By Linda Thurman

Louisiana has hidden treasures—one is the site of the first movie theater in America on Canal Street and another is the team of Ed and Sue Poole, archivists extraordinaire. I was lucky enough to discover both while researching a book about the film industry in Louisiana. A casual remark from Ed about their 20-year struggle to mark the spot took me on a side trip to the past.

In 1896 Americans were cakewalking to "A Hot Time in The Old Town" and marching to "Stars & Stripes Forever" by John Philip Sousa. The novelty of moving images in Vitascope Hall fit the lighthearted mood of the Gay Nineties. Welcome relief from the last few years.

The Gilded Age had ended abruptly with the Panic of 1893, and the country was emerging from the devastating economic crisis that followed. On July 8, 1896, William Jennings Bryan, the Democratic candidate in a bitter presidential campaign, declared "You shall not press down upon the brow of labor this crown of thorns, you shall not crucify mankind upon a cross of gold." Reports said the standing ovation that followed lasted an hour.

New Orleans captured the national spotlight that summer when the U.S. Supreme Court ruled on *Plessy v. Ferguson*. The landmark case upheld Louisiana's "separate but equal" law and would perpetuate segregation until 1954 when *Brown v. Board of Education* changed the national policy.

A corrupt local government was voted out of office and replaced by reformers. The new city council spent 1896 studying the red-light districts in Holland and Germany with the goal of controlling prostitution. New Orleans own

Storyville debuted the following year and would become world-famous as the birthplace of Dixieland and jazz. The ousted politicians moved on to the governor's mansion in the next election.

Meanwhile, 1896 was a leap year and the ladies of New Orleans used the occasion to form "Les Mystérieueses", the first all-women Mardi Gras krewe and the precedent for Venus, Iris and Muses. Local suffragettes were busy founding the Era (Equal Rights Association) Club which successfully lobbied for the right of women to vote on taxation.

No matter their cause or issue that summer, the citizens of New Orleans found themselves on Canal Street, sitting in a darkened room with light flickering on a stretched white canvas. Vitascope Hall drew them all in and gave them precious moments of diversion, laughter, and astonishment. The same reasons we love movies today.

If all goes as planned, the historical marker will be unveiled at 623 Canal Street in 2016. Ed and Sue's drive to mark the forgotten site will be rewarded, thanks to the generosity of Russ and Sandra Herman and the support of Michael Domingue.

This book is the story of how Vitascope Hall came to be and its place in history.

Linda Thurman is the author of Hollywood South: Glamour, Gumbo, and Greed, a Pelican Press Fall 2016 release.

ABOUT THE COVER

The cover features the background of an original circa 1900 early cinema poster (next page) with only the block of text changed. We chose this cover as a tribute for several reasons.

First, because there were no permanent locations for viewing early films, showmen set up temporary movie exhibitions at amusement parks. The original artwork on the poster depicts a turn-of-the-century amusement park, which were quite often located on a waterfront. This would be similar to the situation in New Orleans at West End Park and the other two parks located on the shores of Lake Pontchartrain.

Second, this was an important transition poster. It was not until around 1910 that posters started displaying individual titles. The earliest posters promoted the inventors and their inventions. The next generation of posters became generic and highlighted improvements. This original poster presents the "Latest Edison Fire-Proof Kinetoscope."

Next, the original poster is the oldest in our personal collection. And finally, we chose this cover as a tribute to our poster's history. When the Ford Museum acquired Thomas Edison's office, they found two small stacks of early posters, one from around 1900 and one from around 1903. We were able to trade to get one of each for our personal collection.

ABOUT THE AUTHORS

Ed and Susan Poole
Film Accessory Researchers

For almost 40 years Ed and Susan Poole have been involved with documenting, recording and preserving film accessories (i.e., press books, movie stills, movie posters, general press materials, etc.). Their path has evolved from being just collectors to retail and wholesale dealers and eventually to full time researchers.

Their accomplishments on a national and international level include:

Published the first reference book on movie posters, Collecting Movie Posters, released in 1997 by McFarland Publishers.

Published 19 additional reference books including: Learn About Movie Posters; Learn About International Movie Posters; Movie Still Identification Book; Legality of U.S. Movie Posters; Movie Trailer Identification Codes; National Screen Service Accessory Codes; Production Code Basics; and the Silent Studio Directory.

In 2001, developed the first reference website on movie posters designed for novice to intermediate level collectors: LearnAboutMoviePosters.com.

In 2005, developed the first and only cross referenced research film accessory database with 100,000 images online: MoviePosterDataBase.com.

In 2009, developed the first and only advance research website for documenting press still codes, lithographer plate numbers, etc. – now in a member only research site.

In 2010, the Pooles realized that documentation of local film history was basically non-existent. The Pooles are firm believers that the research and documentation of this history is a necessary foundation for development of many associated industries such as tourism and education.

The Pooles are on a quest to BUILD that foundation for Louisiana through:

Exhibits: In February 2012, the first exhibit on Louisiana Film History was opened at Ellender Memorial Library at Nicholls State University and ran for 4 months during their Jubilee. Since that time, numerous exhibits have been shown throughout the southern part of the state including a 6 month exhibit in the Louisiana section of the State Library of Louisiana.

Film Prints: Some of the most iconic films ever put on the screen have been made in Louisiana. The Pooles have recreated over 75 vintage movie posters on 12"x18" glossy card stock. These are professionally printed and made available to "friends" organizations and fund raising groups to bring more awareness to Louisiana's wonderful film history and to help fund expansion projects to a wider area. You can find these in the *HollywoodOnTheBayou.com* store, in the Historic New Orleans Collection gift shop and several galleries in New Orleans.

Lectures/Presentations: Powerpoint presentations are available on different phases of Louisiana Film History and include clips of vintage film trailers, newspaper clippings and behind the scenes stories plus an exclusive 7 minute documentary on Vitascope Hall (the first seated indoor theater in the U.S. opened in New Orleans in 1896).

Research: Expansion of research information on ALL films made in or about Louisiana is being created and compiled to be available for research students, film makers, industry professionals and the general public. The Pooles have also been actively campaigning for almost 20 years for the placing of markers of the first cinema in the United States which opened in New Orleans in 1896, making Louisiana the Birthplace of the Movie Theater in the United States.

Their research and articles on Louisiana film history have been published in numerous publications such as Louisiana Film and Video (3 times), Arthur Hardy's Mardi Gras Guide, and Point of Vue.

Websites: HollywoodOnTheBayou.com is online and has over 50 vintage Louisiana trailers and lists of Louisiana films by time period AND by Parish. This is a sister site for their larger research websites:

LearnAboutMoviePosters.com;

MoviePosterDataBase.com; and

MovieStillID.com.

Louisiana has now become one of the top film producing states in the U.S. – THAT'S GREAT! Unfortunately, the current political environment is only interested in new production, and Louisiana's film history is being lost, which is tragic.

HOW CAN YOU DEVELOP TOURISM WHEN YOU DON'T KNOW WHAT WAS DONE HERE?

Louisiana has contributed a massive amount to the formation and development of the film industry and WE CAN'T AFFORD to lose our fantastic film history and heritage.

INTRODUCTION

Moving images flickered across a cloth screen: a man sneezing; waves crashing on the shores of Dover; Niagara Falls; the chutes at Coney Island. While today's movie goers would find these scenes laughable, the audiences viewing these less-than-1-minute films in the late 19th century were amazed, astonished, baffled and, in some instances, frightened by the images they were seeing.

In fact, when a scene of a locomotive arriving at a station was shown at an early film exhibition, some members of the crowd, afraid of being crushed by the train bearing down on them, ran away or shrunk into their seats. This was the impact that these early "moving images" had on the 19th century audiences.

This period marked the dawning of the age of the cinema. Early film pioneers could not have foreseen that this "fad," that many believed would eventually lose favor with the public, would turn into an entertainment juggernaut.

So, just how did this industry come about and what is Louisiana's contribution to its growth? That's what **America's First Movie Theater:**

America's First Movie Theater

Louisiana's Vitascope Hall is here to answer.

Although it is generally considered a product of the 19th century, the road to motion pictures actually began thousands of years ago. Through the years, the understanding of optical and vision phenomena grew, leading to the inventions and technologies that ultimately created today's cinema.

Before proceeding to Louisiana's history in the movie industry, it is important to understand the people and inventions that led to it. Credit is given liberally to certain individuals and inventions, depending on the source. Terms like the "first" or the "father of" can vary significantly and can lead to confusion.

The bottom line is that the path to today's movie industry was laid by the contributions of many individuals, some not even acknowledged in today's cinema history.

PRE-CINEMA DEVELOPMENTS

Cinematography is defined simply as the illusion of movement by projecting still pictures in a rapid fashion. Also known as motion pictures, movies or moving pictures, cinematography as we know it today can be traced to the late 19th century. However, its development would not have been possible without certain concepts and technologies that can be traced back thousands of years.

Throughout history, scholars, scientists, and showmen studied and experimented with optical illusions and visual effects. These included discoveries made during this early period in history which paved the way for the inventions that would eventually result in the development of the cinema.

Cave Drawings

The illusion of moving images is based on the optical phenomena known as "persistence of vision" (first described by British physician Peter Mark Roget in 1824) and the "phi phenomenon" (defined by Max Wertheimer in

America's First Movie Theater

1912). Persistence of vision causes the brain to retain images cast upon the retina of the eye for a fraction of a second beyond their disappearance from the field of sight, while the phi phenomenon creates apparent movement between images when they succeed one another rapidly.

An example of these visual principles can be found in early cave drawings where prehistoric people were trying to express movement by painting four pairs of legs on the images with which they decorated their caves.

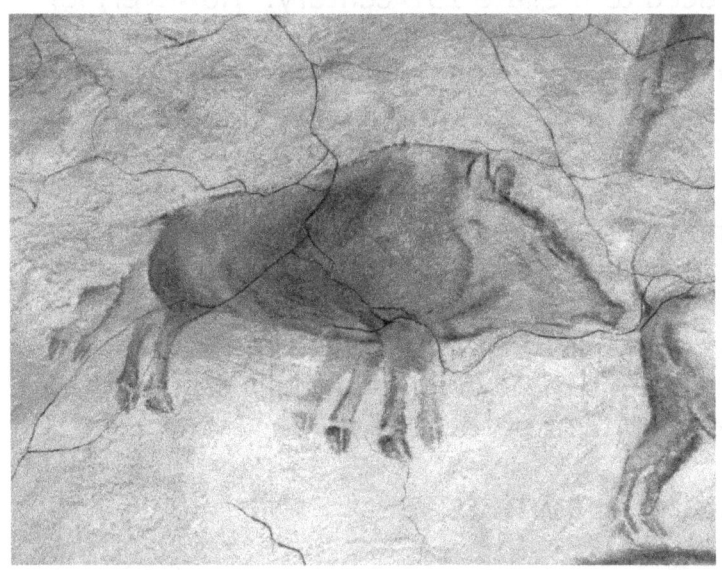

Many scholars believe that the drawing above, discovered in a cave at Altamira, Spain, clearly shows a boar running in a blur with the artist "seeing" more legs than were there.

Magic Lantern

In the 1600s, various European inventors developed simple devices for projecting imagery using a light source, mirror, and lens apparatus. Technological advances such as the invention of the telescope and microscope were made in the field of optics during this era, which also benefitted magic lanterns.

Though its originator is still debated, recent research has indicated that a form of "magic lantern" may have existed in the time of Solomon. Aristotle developed the theoretical basis of the science of optics. With Friar Roger Bacon, born in 1214, the art-science of light and shadow reached a point at which magic shadow entertainment devices could be built. Leonardo da Vinci invented the "bulls-eye" lens, a primitive but effective condenser.

By the 1660's, optical lanterns were exhibited regularly in cities across Europe by individuals like the Dutch physicist Christian Huygens, Danish mathematician Thomas Rasmussen Walgensten, and British optician Richard Reeves. It soon became a showman's instrument.

By the end of the century, wandering lanternists were putting on small-scale shows in inns and castles, using a lantern lit with a candle. Often these shows featured goblins and devils -- hence the name the "magic lantern."

By the end of the 19th and the early 20th centuries, magic-lanterns were everywhere -- in homes, churches, fraternal lodges, schools, large-scale halls and theaters, and as a regular part of home and public entertainment.

Magic lanterns came in all sizes and shapes, from toy lanterns for children to those used in large halls -- huge brass-and-mahogany, double-lens machines lit with "limelight."

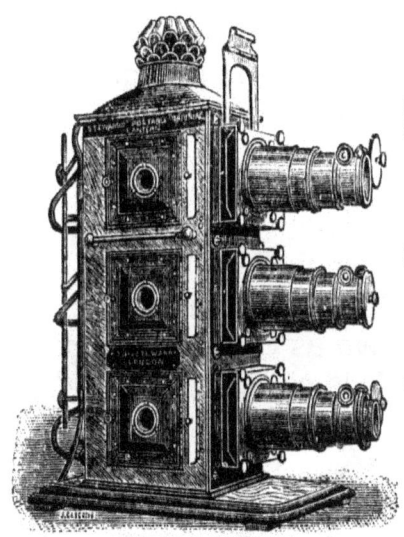

TRIPLE LANTERNS,
Prices from £25 to £100.

MAGIC LANTERNS
AND
Dissolving View Apparatus,
SLIDES, AND EFFECTS,
Of the Highest Class.

GOLD & SILVER MEDALS AWARDED (1884-5)
For Optical and Mechanical excellence.

Sole Maker of the Registered
TRIPLE LANTERN,
The Luke Bi-unial Lanterns,
And the 3-Wick Paraffine
PHOTOGENIC LANTERNS.
Prices—£3:10:0 to £10:10:0.

ILLUSTRATED CATALOGUES gratis, post-free to all parts of the World.

406, 66, & 456, STRAND; 54, CORNHILL, LONDON.

Photography

Developments in still photography also aided the creation of movies. Here are two of these key developments.

Joseph Niépce (1765-1833) (next page) was a French inventor usually credited as the inventor of photography and a pioneer in that

America's First Movie Theater

field. He developed heliography, a technique he used to create the world's oldest surviving product of a photographic process: a print made from a photoengraved printing plate in 1825.

In 1827, he used a primitive camera to produce the oldest surviving photograph of a real-world scene, known as the View from a Window at Le Gras. This photograph took nearly eight hours to expose.

In 1839, Henry Fox Talbot (1800-1877) (right) made an important advancement in photograph production with the introduction of negatives on paper - as opposed to glass. Also around this time, it became possible to print photographic images on glass slides which could be projected using magic lanterns.

Optical Toys

The early experiments with optical toys such as the Thaumatrope (next page), Phenakistoscope and the Zoetrope showed that moving pictures could be generated from a series of static images.

In 1825, John Ayrton Paris (1785-1856) (left), an English physician, invented the Thaumatrope, a Victorian optical toy. Although the invention has also been attributed to John Herschel and Charles Babbage, amongst others, it was Paris who was the first to distribute it commercially.

It was constructed from a simple disk or card featuring a different picture on each side and attached to two pieces of string. When the strings are twirled rapidly the card rotates on its axis and the two images appear to combine.

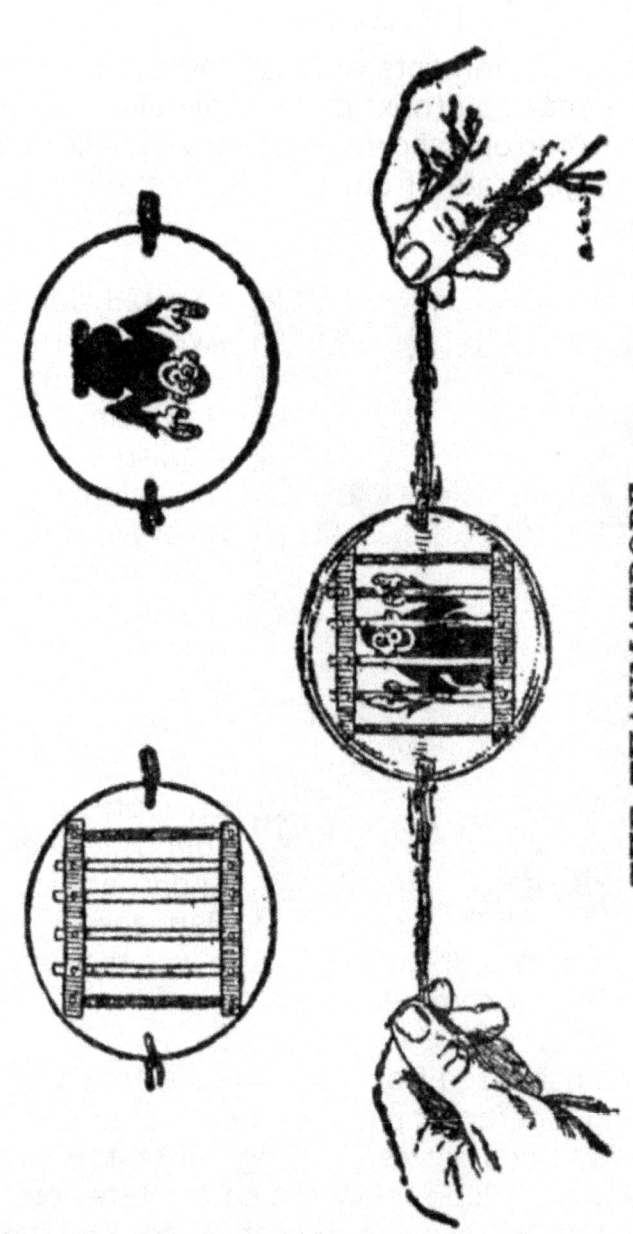

THE THAUMATROPE.

Above: How the designs of the two sides are placed with respect to each other.
Below: The combined image when the thaumatrope is twirled.

In 1832, Joseph Plateau (left) and sons introduced the Phenakistoscope (next page), also known as the Fantoscope. The Phenakistoscope was based on the persistence of motion principle which creates an illusion of motion.

Like other optical toys of its kind, the Phenakistoscope was one of the more successful illusion toys. It had two disks with the inner disk holding the pictures in order on the rim, and the outside disk which the viewer (one at a time) looked through.

The outer disks had blackened slits to ensure a constant clear frame and to shield unwanted light off the picture once seen. Both turned on the identical axis. When turned together, the impression of motion was achieved.

After going to market, the Phenakistoscope received other names, including Phantasmascope and Fantoscope (and Phenakistiscope in Britain and many other countries). It was quite successful for two years until 1834.

America's First Movie Theater

In that year, William George Horner (left) invented the Zoetrope, which offered two improvements on the Phenakistoscope. First, the zoetrope did not require a viewing mirror. The second and most influential improvement was that more than one person could view the moving pictures at the same time.

The Zoetrope (below) or Daedelum was a horizontally rotating drum (about 12 inches in diameter) which held pictures of different sorts on the inner rim. These pictures showed forms in successive stages of forward motion.

America's First Movie Theater

On the outer rim were equally spaced slits which the viewer looked through. As the drum is spun at speeds reaching 14 frames per seconds, the figures appear to perform natural movements.

T. H. McALLISTER, OPTICIAN, 49 NASSAU STREET, N. Y.

ZOETROPE.

The **ZOETROPE, or "Wheel of Life,"** is an instructive Scientific Toy, illustrating in an attractive manner the persistence of an image on the retina of the eye; it consists of a card-board cylinder, about 12 inches diameter, and 8 inches deep, with 13 equidistant narrow openings, each about 3 inches long, arranged near the top as shown in the engraving. The lower end rests on an iron shaft, rising from a substantial wood base; on strips of paper, about 3¼ inches wide, 36 inches long, are printed figures of men, animals. etc., in different positions, which are placed in the cylinder. By revolving the cylinder by the hand, and looking through the openings, the images passing rapidly before the eye are blended, so as to give the figures the motions of life in the most natural manner. As many persons as can stand around the Zoetrope can see the movements at the same time.

PRICE OF THE ZOETROPE, $2.50.

Including following series of 12 amusing pictures: Base-ball Player, Chewing Gum, Dolphin Swimming, Donnybrook Fair, Gymnast, Hash Machine, Jig Dancer, Johnny Jumper, Keep the Ball Rolling, Kick her up, Old Dog Tray, Raining Pitchforks.

CINEMA PIONEERS

Contrary to popular belief, the film industry was not developed in the United States by a single individual. It was the product of a number of inventors from many countries over several decades.

In the late 1800s, the United States was not the economic powerhouse that it is today. At that time, England was the world's economic center and London was the largest city in the world.

All international trade went through England. This allowed them to see new inventions earlier than anyone else. And there were tons of them – from many countries –trying to invent a camera/projector of moving images. These inventors and their creations would ultimately lead to the cinema known today.

While there were many inventors working on cameras and projectors, the following gentlemen are most commonly credited with creating today's motion picture industry.

Eadweard Muybridge

Known by some as the "father of the motion picture," British emigrant Eadweard Muybridge's (right) early photographic experiments laid a foundation for modern cinema. Muybridge's *The Horse In Motion* (1882) is regarded by many as the first ever moving picture. (See image next page)

In the 1870s, Muybridge experimented with instantaneously recording the movements of a galloping horse at a Sacramento, California race track. As Muybridge's reputation as a photographer grew in the late 1800s, former California Governor Leland Stanford contacted him to help settle a bet.

Speculation had raged for years over whether all four hooves of a running horse left the ground at the same time. Stanford believed they did, but the motion was too fast for the human eye to detect.

In 1872, Muybridge began photographing a galloping horse in a sequence of shots. His initial findings appeared to indicate that the governor was right. Unfortunately, due to imperfections in Muybridge's methods, it could not be confirmed with certainty.

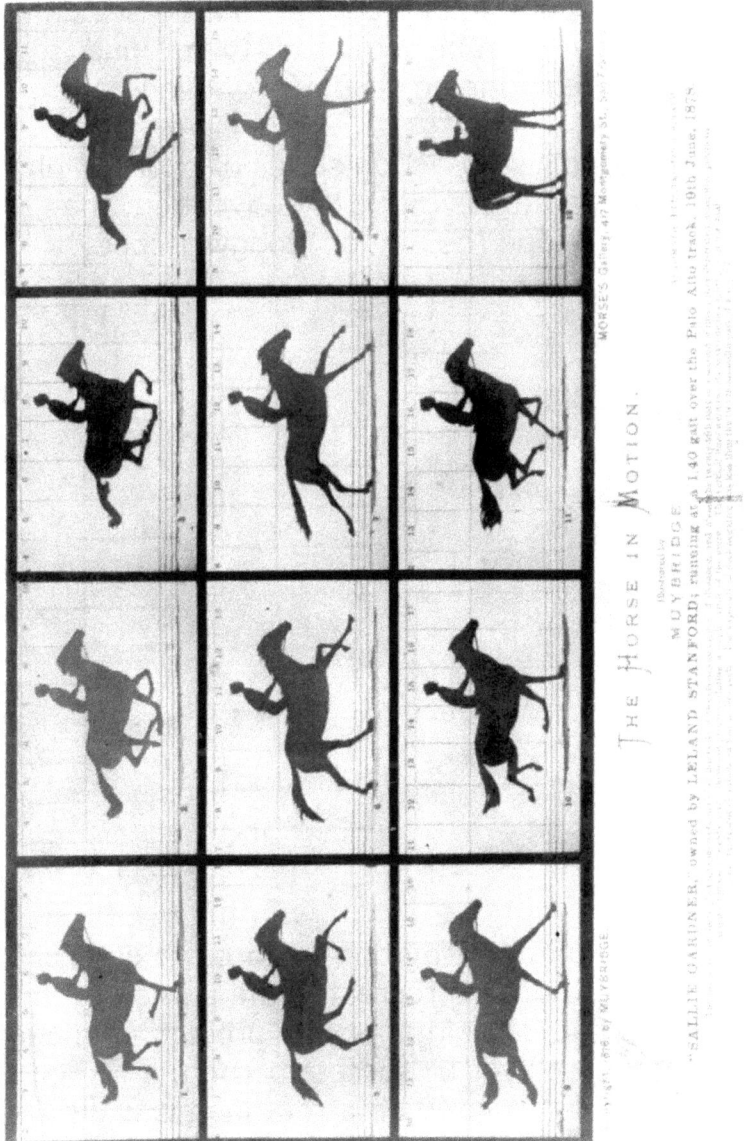

America's First Movie Theater

With further funding from Stanford, however, Muybridge eventually devised a more complex method of photographing horses in motion. By 1879, Muybridge had proven that horses do at times have all four hooves off the ground during their running stride (preceding page).

Muybridge's stop-action series of photographs helped lead to his own 1879 invention, the Zoopraxiscope (below) or "zoogyroscope."

It was a primitive motion-picture projector machine that also recreated the illusion of movement (or animation) by projecting images rapidly displayed in succession onto a screen from photos printed on a rotating glass disc.

Charles Emile Reynaud

French-born Charles-Emile Reynaud (left) developed a technical understanding of visual science as a photographer's apprentice. In 1876, he made an optical toy to amuse a young child (below).

Improving on the Phenakistiscope (invented by Joseph Plateau) and the Zoetrope (developed by William George Horner), Reynaud invented

America's First Movie Theater

the Praxinoscope (below) which was patented on December 21, 1877.

It consisted of a cylinder and a strip of paper showing twelve frames for animation. As the cylinder rotated, stationary mirrors in the center revealed a "single image" in motion. The result was perfect animation without the loss of luminosity in movement which was experienced with the Zoetrope.

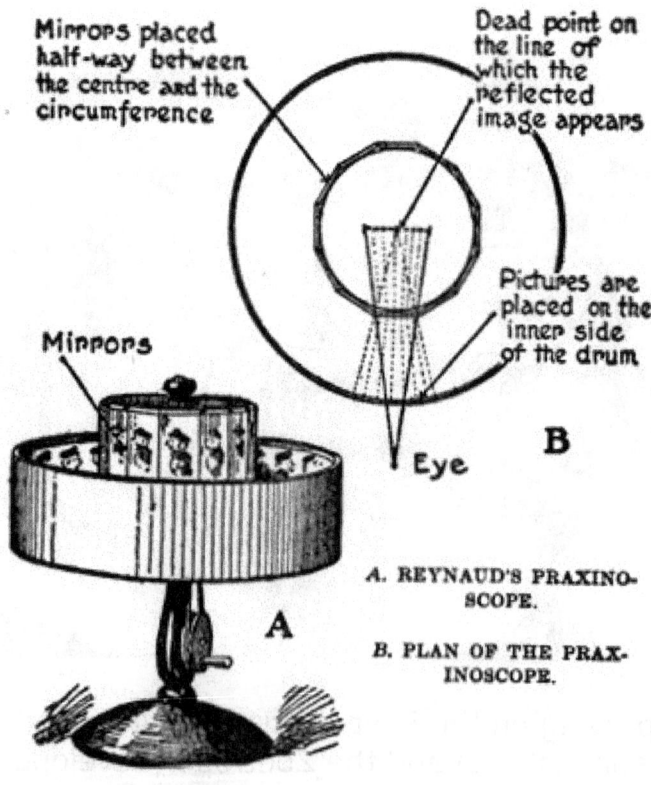

A. REYNAUD'S PRAXINO-SCOPE.

B. PLAN OF THE PRAXINOSCOPE.

The next step, as Reynaud saw it, was to adapt his existing device so that the animated pictures could be projected. In December 1888 Reynaud patented his Théâtre Optique (below), a large-scale Praxinoscope intended for public projection.

By using spools to feed and take-up the extended picture band, sequences were no longer limited to short cyclic movements. The images were painted on gelatin squares and fastened between leather bands, with holes in metal strips between the pictures engaging in pins on the revolving wheel, so that each picture was aligned with a facet of the mirror drum. This was the first commercial use of the perforations that were to be so important for successful cinematography.

America's First Movie Theater

On October 20, 1892 Reynaud premiered "Pauvre Pierrot" at his "Theatre Optique." The presentation was the very first exhibition of moving pictures shown publicly via projection onto a screen.

Etienne-Jules Marey

True motion pictures, rather than eye-fooling animations, could only occur after the development of film (flexible and transparent celluloid) that could record split-second pictures. Some of the first experiments in this regard were conducted by Parisian innovator and physiologist Etienne-Jules Marey in the 1880s (above).

Marey was also studying, experimenting, and recording bodies (most often of flying animals, such as pelicans in flight) in motion using photographic means (and French astronomer Pierre-Jules-Cesar Janssen's "revolving photographic plate" idea).

Marey, claimed by some to be the "inventor of cinema," constructed a camera (or "photographic gun") that could take multiple (12) photographs per second of moving animals or humans (next page). It was called chronophotography or serial photography, similar to Muybridge's work on taking multiple exposed images of running horses. He was able to record multiple images of a subject's movement on the same camera plate, rather than the individual images Muybridge had produced.

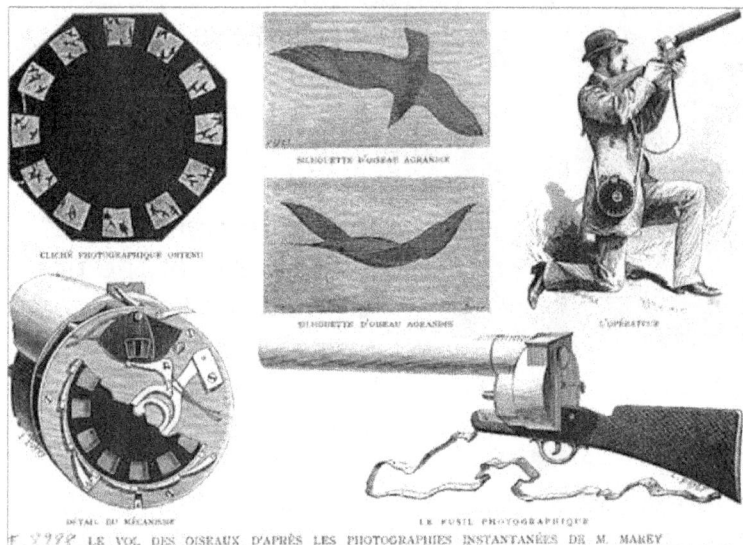

The modern cinematic term "shooting a film" was possibly derived from Marey's invention.

Louis Aimé Augustin Le Prince

The life of this little known but significant film pioneer is as strange as any stories told on the silver screen. French-born Le Prince (right) shot the first moving pictures on paper film using a single lens camera. He has been heralded by some as the "Father of Cinematography" since 1930. Le Prince spent time in both the

United States and England.

In 1886, during his time in the States, Le Prince built a camera that used 16 different lenses to capture motion (below).

Though the projected image was quite jerky, it earned Le Prince his first patent.

America's First Movie Theater

In 1887, Le Prince returned to the United Kingdom and in May, designed and built a single lens camera (below).

America's First Movie Theater

In October of 1888, Le Prince used his invention to shoot and record *Roundhay Garden Scene* (below) on an Eastman Kodak 1885 paper-based photographic film. The film is considered by some to be the world's first motion picture. Though just seconds long, this and another movie, *Leeds Bridge*, are the oldest existing movies in the world, shot well before Thomas Edison or the Lumiere brothers even had a working camera.

Le Prince was planning to patent his camera in the UK and then promote it publicly in New York. But before he did, he decided to go home to France to visit family and friends. On September 16, 1890 Le Prince boarded an express train bound for Paris in Dijon in eastern France. Although he had promised he would rejoin his friends in Paris for a return journey to England, he was never seen again.

The last sighting of Le Prince was onboard the train. His luggage, stored in a separate compartment, was also never seen again.

Not long afterwards, Thomas Edison tried to take credit as the inventor of cinematography. Understandably, Louis Le Prince's wife Elizabeth and son Adolphe were keen to advance Le Prince's cause as inventor.

Adolphe Le Prince appeared as a witness for the defense in a court case brought by Thomas Edison against the American Mutoscope Company claiming that Edison was the first and sole inventor of cinematography. Adolphe was not allowed to present his father's two cameras as evidence and eventually the court ruled in favor of Edison. A year later that ruling was overturned.

When competing inventors such as Edison and the Lumière brothers developed the ability to create similar films, they were the ones to receive the fame as motion picture pioneers.

Though both French police and Scotland Yard carried out an exhaustive search for his body and luggage, neither was ever found and the case remains unsolved today. Le Prince was officially declared dead in 1897.

Because he shot his films on paper-based film, the *Roundhay Garden Scene* as well as *Leeds*

Bridge and *The Accordion Player* have survived and remain proof of Le Prince's contribution to the cinema.

Thomas Edison and William Kennedy Laurie Dickson

Thomas Edison (below), inventor of the phonograph cylinder in 1877, had been following the success of other inventors in the motion picture industry. In 1888, Edison set out to build a device that "does for the eye what the phonograph has done for the ear." This meant reproducing recorded visual movement in an inexpensive and practical way.

America's First Movie Theater

Eadward Muybridge, inventor of the Zoopraxiscope, approached Edison about collaborating on a new projector but this never materialized. Instead, after Muybridge left, Edison and his assistant William Kennedy Laurie Dickson began experimenting with adapting the phonograph and tried in vain to make rows of tiny photographs on similar cylinders.

Dickson (left) had heard about a new transparent celluloid film developed by Hannibal W. Goodwin and manufactured by George Eastman. Dickson wanted to try the celluloid and ordered the first samples in 35mm, establishing the size that continued as the industry standard. Dickson and his team at the Edison lab then worked on the development of a motion picture exhibition device utilizing the celluloid film.

The prototype, which they called the Kinetoscope (next page), consisted of a cabinet with approximately 50' of film on spools. Patrons would turn a crank (which moved the spools of film) while viewing through a peephole.

America's First Movie Theater

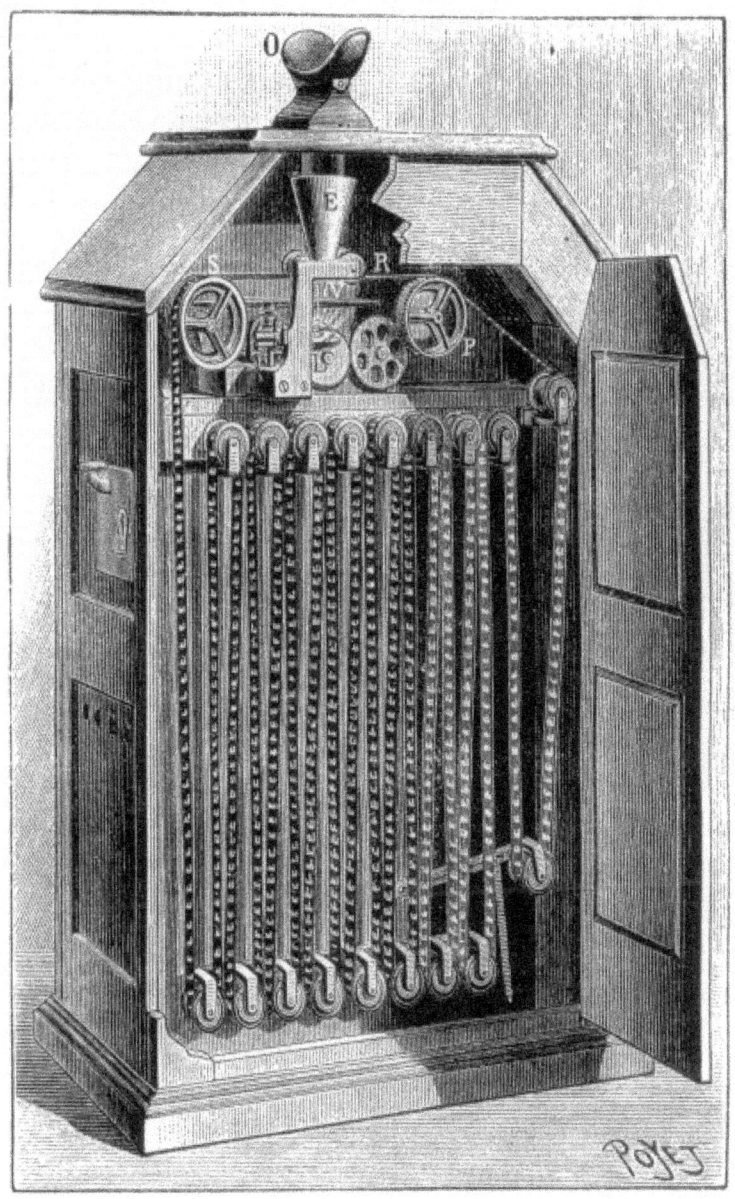

America's First Movie Theater

On May 20, 1891, Edison and Dickson debuted the Kinetoscope (below) at a convention of the National Federation of Women's Clubs. Edison filed for patent rights for his new device and held a public demonstration at the Brooklyn Institute of Arts and Sciences on May 9, 1893.

America's First Movie Theater

On April 14, 1894, a commercial version of the *Kinetoscope* was placed into the first "parlors" owned by the Holland Brothers, at 1155 Broadway, in New York City. It became an instant success with other parlors following (below).

Auguste and Louis Lumiere

By the early 1890s, French brothers Auguste and Louis Lumiere (below) had built their family business into the biggest manufacturers of photographic plates in Europe. Inspired by an exhibition of the Kinetoscope, the Lumière brothers began working on a process to combine film recording and projection into a single device.

The brothers identified the two main problems with Edison's Kinetoscope as its bulk and the issue of only one viewer being able to observe the scene at a time.

America's First Movie Theater

To solve these problems, the brothers invented the Cinematographe (below), a device combining a camera with a printer and projector as well as the function to produce intermittent movement in order to display motion pictures for an audience.

Le cinématographe Lumière: projection.

America's First Movie Theater

The device was lightweight, operated by a hand crank, and available for multiple viewers to watch at one time. The Cinematographe was patented in February of 1895 and a month later, they screened their first short film, *La Sortie des ouvriers de l'usine Lemiére*, which depicted workers leaving a factory. It was considered by some as the first motion picture.

RISE OF THE AMERICAN CINEMA

The success of the Lumiere's Cinematographe had an almost immediate impact on the American film industry.

By 1895, sales of Edison's Kinetoscope began to decline, due in part to the introduction of the Lumiere projector in the United States. While the Kinetoscope was a "peep show" style

America's First Movie Theater

cabinet designed for one viewer, the Lumiere's projector could be seen by a large crowd.

Edison's main objective at this time was to use the Kinetoscope as a vehicle to promote his phonograph cylinder. So convinced that movies were a passing fancy, Edison did not file for international patents on the Kinetoscope and related equipment, although he did sell the rights for international distribution.

William Dickson wanted to move on from the individual "peepshow" style and develop a mechanism designed for exhibiting to an audience. Thomas Edison, however, thought that moving picture exhibitions were a temporary fad, and that projecting them on a large screen would exhaust the novelty. Edison's newly appointed general manager, W.E. Gilmore, also wanted to continue selling the Kinetoscope, which irked Dickson.

During this time, a former Edison employee, Eugene Lauste, asked Dickson for help on a problem he was having at his new job with Grey and Otway Latham. Lauste, a French engineer, had been hired by Edison to assist Dickson in developing a connection between Edison's sound cylinder and the Kinetoscope.

After Lauste left the employ of Edison, he went to work for the Lathams to help with the development of the first wide screen projector called the Eidoloscope (below).

America's First Movie Theater

Lauste gained notoriety for his invention which revolutionized the film industry. It was dubbed the "Latham Loop."

Edison's manager Gilmore heard about Dickson helping Lauste and considered it a betrayal, and immediately communicated his feelings to Edison. After an argument over the situation, Dickson left Edison's employ in April of 1895.

After working briefly with the Lathams, Dickson turned his attention to development work for the KMCD group (Koopman, Marvin, Casler, Dickson) which he and three friends had set up at the end of 1894. The group incorporated the American Mutoscope Company in New Jersey in December 1895.

The firm manufactured the Mutoscope (next page), and made flip-card movies for it, as a rival to Edison's Kinetoscope for individual "peep shows," making the company Edison's chief competitor in the nickelodeon market.

In the summer of 1896, Biograph introduced a projector capable of exhibiting movies to a large crowd and Dickson and Edison would go head-to-head in the projection market (page 42).

America's First Movie Theater

The Mutoscope

For Pennies A Moving Picture Machine

The MUTOSCOPE AND — HOW IT MAKES MONEY.

Size, 4 feet, 8 inches high.   Shipping weight, 325 pounds
Very popular in all public places

America's First Movie Theater

The Phantoscope

In 1894, Frank R. Gammon and Norman C. Raff, Ohio businessmen, were granted exclusive domestic rights to the Kinetoscope. In 1895, they urged Edison to design and manufacture a projector based upon the principle of his camera, feeding the film intermittently so as to secure satisfactory illumination.

The work was underway when Edison met two inventors from the Washington, D.C. area. This meeting changed Edison's direction and brought about the creation of America's cinema – and Louisiana's connection.

America's First Movie Theater

Charles Francis Jenkins and Thomas Armat together invented one of the most effective motion picture projectors of their day. They gave a commercial public film screening of their new invention in September 1895. It was known as The Phantoscope, a name which had been given to a number of earlier prototypes.

Charles Francis Jenkins (below) was a stenographer in the Life Saving Service of the U.S. Treasury Department (today known as the U.S. Coast Guard).

In 1890, the young inventor began the creation of a movie projector. In his spare time, Jenkins had been working on what he

America's First Movie Theater

referred to as a "motion picture projecting box." He named it a Phantoscope (below), as he did with all of his early motion picture inventions.

In an interview appearing in *Transactions of the Society of Motion Picture Engineers*, Issues 8-14, Jenkins stated:

> Exhibitions to friends were given from time to time in 1891, 1892 and 1893, though my first exhibition of which any account appeared in printed publications, was in June of 1894.

This documented event occurred at 726 East Main Street in Richmond, Indiana, just a few miles south of his boyhood home.

The *Richmond Telegram* reported the following:

America's First Movie Theater

All morning Charles made ready to show his friends the object that had been the center of his attention for two years ... He needed electrical current to run it but there was no electricity in the store. The source of the purposed illumination was from a large-bowled lamp. The only current in reach was a trolley wire that passed the door on Main Street. To this Jenkins attached a lateral wire and brought it down to the proper voltage by means of a pail of water. He placed the machine on the counter and hung a bed sheet on the opposite wall. The window blinds were drawn on passersby on Main while the young man's father and mother together with a few friends and newsmen stood in half-light wondering what was about to be revealed."

There began a sputtering sound as the machine kicked into life and out of the lens shot light onto the wall and a girl clad in garments more picturesque than protective stepped lively. She did not seem bashful thus displayed, while those in the audience were taken aback. She was "Annabelle", a vaudeville favorite, who had been engaged by young Jenkins for a special performance in the backyard of his Washington boarding house. With the audience consisting of him and his

America's First Movie Theater

camera, Jenkins had captured her for posterity while she executed the intricacies of a butterfly dance. The lady's remunerations for interpreting the insect's terpsichorean movements had been five dollars, which seemed to cover adequately all the artistry displayed, although her costume was of a far briefer coverage... As the sputtering grew louder and the grinding more fervid the girl began to reproduce on the wall the movements she had executed in the boarding house backyard which were ... of a twirling dervish variety ..."

As the last arc ceased to sputter and the window-shades rolled up, the people began to ask one another what they had seen. It was not certainly clear. Although there had been the gesticulating girl ... from where had she come? How did she move? The viewers went behind the screen to impress the wall and ascertain there was no trickery, for there were no words to express it.

This is believed to be the earliest documented projection of a motion picture before an audience. The *Photographic Times* and *The New York Herald Tribune* also documented the premier.

America's First Movie Theater

In the winter of 1894, while attending the Bliss School of Electricity in Washington, Jenkins was introduced by Mr. Bliss to Thomas Armat.

Armat (left) was also an inventor, having already obtained patents for an automatic car-coupler and a conduit electric railway system. In the summer of 1894, Armat saw the first exhibition of the Edison Kinetoscope in Washington.

H. A. Tabb, a childhood friend who was also acquainted with Raff and Gammon, exclusive agents for the Kinetoscope, approached Armat about financing future exhibitions. One of the places Tabb had in mind for a profitable exhibition was the Cotton States Exposition scheduled for the following year.

In a letter written to the *Journal of the Society of Motion Picture Engineers* in 1935, Armat said that after investigating the matter, he could not see anything very promising about the Kinetoscope as a commercial project, but that he could see potential if the pictures could be projected upon a screen. Tabb's answer was that he did not believe it was possible to

America's First Movie Theater

project such pictures successfully, because he knew that Raff and Gammon had urged the Edison Company to produce such a machine and they failed to do so.

Armat indicated that he believed it was possible and began research to accomplish a way of projecting such pictures upon a screen and starting preparations for experimental work.

Armat enrolled as a student in the Bliss School, largely for the purpose of acquiring practical information as to handling an arc light that he wanted to use in his projector. When Armat explained his purpose to Professor Bliss, he introduced him to Jenkins who was also interested in motion picture experiments.

In Jenkins' book, *The Boyhood of an Inventor*, he described his new partner as "a junior member of a real estate firm in Washington."

Armat and Jenkins entered into a written agreement on March 25, 1895 which clearly stated that Armat would "finance and promote the invention" of Jenkins. The two worked together to make improvements to the Phantoscope and a joint patent was applied for on August 28, 1895 (next page).

America's First Movie Theater

(No Model.) 2 Sheets—Sheet 2.
C. F. JENKINS & T. ARMAT.
PHANTOSCOPE.
No. 586,953. Patented July 20, 1897.

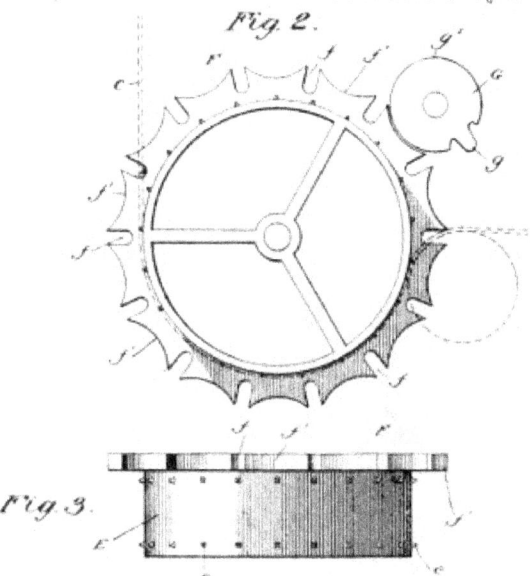

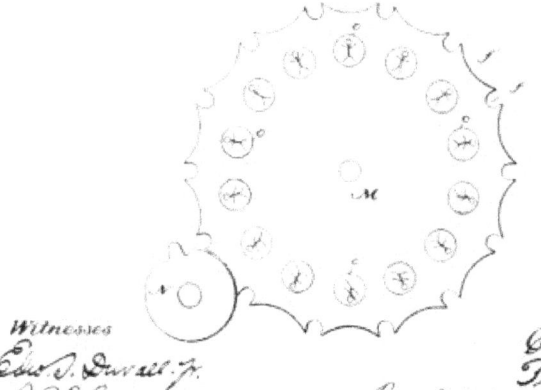

America's First Movie Theater

In September of 1895, the duo took three of their machines (below) to the 1895 Cotton States and International Exposition held at the current Piedmont Park in Atlanta, Georgia (called the 100 Day Expo).

The exposition was designed to promote the region to the world and showcase products and new technologies as well as to encourage trade with Latin America. It featured exhibits from several states including various innovations in agriculture and technology.

Armat and Jenkins, who secured the last space available, obtained a concession from the Exposition authorities that allowed them to build a temporary two-room theater exhibit booth which was located at the far eastern end of the Midway, next to the Old Plantation Show. They charged $.25 for a viewing, hoping that the receipts would help to pay the exploitation expenses.

America's First Movie Theater

America's First Movie Theater

The *Baltimore Sun* of October 3 reported on this event:

> The last concession of space made by the Atlanta Exposition management before the opening of the big Cotton States show will be occupied by the machine that Edison has been working years to perfect. There is no Edison in this, however. The Wizard of Menlo Park has been beaten at his own game by two young Washingtonians. Baltimore Sun, October 3, 1895, p. 103)

Two weeks into the Expo, things were not going as brisk as they had hoped. Jenkins eventually left the Exposition and took one of the three Phantoscopes to his brother's wedding in Richmond, Indiana. Films were then shown at his father's jewelry store, and according to the *Richmond Daily Times*, "Those fortunate enough to see them were enraptured at the wonderful and beautiful effects seen."

While still in Atlanta, Armat experienced unexpected difficulties. On October 15, a fire erupted in the adjacent "Old Plantation Show" and badly damaged the partners' exhibit. Discouraged by the damage and the poor box-office receipts, Armat soon closed the booth and left.

America's First Movie Theater

The anticipated Exposition crowds did not materialize, the receipts were small, and a very considerable loss was incurred. According to Jenkins, "The exhibition, itself, was a very successful one," but there were few patrons.

The problem was primarily one of promotion. The Cotton States Exposition attracted other people in the moving picture field. Gray Latham was there with the Eidoloscope and Frank Harrison represented Raff & Gammon's Kinetoscope Company with its peephole machines.

Latham's and Harrison's exhibits were located in the technology areas. Since Armat and Jenkins were the last exhibitors to get a booth, they were left out of the program, which had already been printed. In addition, they were set in an area of live performances and live exhibits on the back side of the Expo.

After Armat and Jenkins returned home, the two had a falling out, each claiming ownership of the Phantoscope. The U.S. Patent Office granted Jenkins a patent for his initial projector and Jenkins and Armat a patent for the modified version (both were named Phantoscopes). Armat purchased Jenkins' interest in the jointly-patented camera.

Vitascope

After the split with Jenkins, Armat made several revisions to the Phantoscope (below). One change was the addition of a sprocket wheel in the upper part of the machine, incorporating the "Latham Loop." Armat then approached agents Raff and Gammon about manufacturing his improved projector.

America's First Movie Theater

The agents were excited by what they saw and contacted Edison about developing the equipment. Edison agreed to purchase and manufacture the Phantoscope projector on the condition that he could rename it and call it his own invention.

In December 1895, Armat started negotiations with Raff and Gammon and shortly thereafter entered into a contract with them. Under the terms as stated, Raff and Gammon were to supply Edison films for use on the "Vitascope," the name Armat had originally given the projector as described in his patent. For their part, Edison Manufacturing Company would obtain a certain number of the projectors.

Raff and Gammon wanted to use the Edison name in connection with their exploitation of the Vitascope, for obvious commercial reasons. They also wanted to be assured of a continued supply of Edison films. Armat and Edison agreed. Henceforth, the machine was known as "Edison's Vitascope." (image on the next page)

Once the name was settled, Raff and Gammon turned their attention to marketing and profit maximization. Potential investors as well as potential audiences were waiting for the screen machine that Edison had promised them many times before. Commercial exhibitions of

America's First Movie Theater

projected motion pictures by non-Edison showmen had already been given but without notable success.

Edison's Vitascope made its first theatrical exhibition on April 23, 1896, at Koster and Bial's Music Hall in New York City. The vaudeville circuit was a fitting venue because it not only provided a ready audience but also a source for film subjects including Annabelle, the "butterfly dancer" and the theatrical production of "A Milk White Flag."

During the premiere, film was projected onto a screen set within a gilt frame to create literally a "moving picture" for an amazed audience.

EDISON'S LATEST TRIUMPH.

Vitascope to Cast Figures on Canva. at Koster & Bial's.

Thomas A. Edison and Albert Bial have perfected arrangements by which Edison's latest invention, the vitascope, will be exhibited for the first time anywhere at Koster & Bial's Music Hall. Edison has been at work on the vitascope for several years.

The vitascope projects upon a large area of canvas groups that appear to stand forth from the canvas, and move with great facility and agility, as though actuated by separate impulses. In this way the bare canvas before the audience becomes instantly a stage upon which living beings move about.

Mr. Bial said yesterday: "I propose to reproduce in this way at Koster & Bial's scenes from various successful plays, and operas of the season, and well-known statesmen and celebrities will be represented, as, for instance, making a speech or performing some important act or series of acts with which their names are identified. No other manager in this city will have the right to exhibit the vitascope."

America's First Movie Theater

The reception for the new and improved Vitascope was excellent.

America's First Movie Theater

The next day, *The New York Times* reported on the event:

EDISON'S VITASCOPE CHEERED.

"Projecting Kinetoscope" Exhibited for First Time at Koster & Bial's.

The new thing at Koster & Bial's last night was Edison's vitascope, exhibited for the first time. The ingenious inventor's latest toy is a projection of is kinetoscope figures, in stereopticon fashion, upon a white screen in a darkened hall. In the centre of the balcony of the big music hall is a curious object, which looks from below like the double turret of a big monitor. In the front of each half of it are two oblong holes. The turret is neatly covered with the blue velvet brocade which is the favorite decorative material in this house. The white screen used on the stage is framed like a picture. The moving figures are about half life size.

When the hall was darkened last night a buzzing and roaring were heard in the turret, and an unusually bright light fell upon the screen. Then came into view two precious blond young persons of the variety stage, in pink and blue dresses, doing the umbrella dance with

America's First Movie Theater

commendable celebrity. Their motions were all clearly defined. When they vanished, a view of an angry surf breaking on a sandy beach near a stone pier amazed the spectators. The waves tumbled in furiously and the foam of the breakers flew high in the air. A burlesque boxing match between a tall, thin comedian and a short, fat one, a comic allegory called "The Monroe Doctrine"; an instant of motion in Hoyt's farce, A Milk White Flag," repeated over and over again, and a skirt dance by a tall blonde completed the views, which were all wonderfully real and singularly exhilarating. For the spectator's imagination filled the atmosphere with electricity, as sparks crackled around the swiftly moving, lifelike figures.

So enthusiastic was the appreciation of the crowd long before the extraordinary exhibition was finished that vociferous cheering was heard. There were loud calls for Mr. Edison, but he made no response.

With the success of the premiere of his new equipment, Edison was ready to start licensing territories through Raff & Gammon. They were overrun with orders for state rights.

America's First Movie Theater

ROCK & WAINWRIGHT PURCHASE LOUISIANA RIGHTS

The successful exhibition of Edison's Vitascope created an immediate interest in the new projector and territories sold quickly.

Raff & Gammon
(ORGANIZERS OF THE KINETOSCOPE CO.)

EXCLUSIVE CONTROL OF THE
LATEST MARVEL

The Vitascope

SOLE AGENTS FOR THE
EDISON KINETOSCOPE
IN THE UNITED STATES AND CANADA
THE EDISON PHONOGRAPH

PHONOGRAPH AND KINETOSCOPE SUPPLIES,
ELECTRIC DESIGNS, ETC

Postal Telegraph Building, 253 Broadway
Removed to 43 W. 28th St.,
New York.

Vitascope opened Keiths Theatre
May 4th — Boston, Mass

N. C. R.
Harry Brooks, Esq.,
2995 Washington St.
Roxbury, Mass.
Dear Sir:-
    Replying to your postal card of the 5th inst., we beg to say that the right to Massachusetts has been sold, and if you wish to exhibit in that state, you will have to address the purchaser, Mr. P. W. Kiefaber, 419 New Market St., Philadelphia, Pa.
    Would be glad to sell you the right to any state remaining open, but they are nearly all taken, and you should act promptly if you wish to secure such a right.
                Very truly yours,

America's First Movie Theater

Two of the last investors in the new enterprise were an Englishman named William T. Rock (below) and his partner Walter Wainwright.

William T. "Pop" Rock was born in Birmingham, England, on December 31, 1853, and remained there during his boyhood. After attending public schools, he came to America as a young man. He began working for a circus company, giving him his first experience as a showman.

America's First Movie Theater

From the beginning of his career in America, he displayed keen judgment in selecting promising enterprises and always was on the watch for something new. Having acquired considerable capital in the early 1880's, he became proprietor of the Madison Hotel in New York City. In 1886, Rock, along with Edward Purvis and Michael Crane, formed the Ball Electric Illuminating Company where Rock served as president.

In an interview appearing in the *Moving Picture World* trade magazine, Rock explained how he became involved with the Vitascope.

> *My start in the picture business was made in 1896; it was this way: Raff & Gammon, then doing business at 43 West Twenty-eighth Street, New York City, had the state rights for the Edison Vitascope Projector.*
>
> *At that time, I was handling a line of arc lamps, and engaged by them to do some electrical work on their premises.*
>
> *While I was there, they suggested it would be a good investment for me to take one of the states on the Vitascope, but the best they had left was Louisiana, which they held at $2,500. In fact, if I rightly remember, it was the only state left.*

America's First Movie Theater

> *After some hesitation I entered into a partnership with Walter Wainwright, a close friend, and we took the state at the figure named.*

Walter Wainwright was a tight wire walker (billed as "King of the Wire") and carnival showman known professionally as "Wainretta."

Wainwright was looking forward to making his fortune in the new industry, risking his circus career and financial security to do so.

The firm of Rock & Wainwright was established and the partnership stocked up with films and headed south.

In his interview, Rock continued his story:

> *Before doing this we made sure we could obtain the services of a man, William Reed, who could handle the projection end of the venture, as several buyers of state rights were experiencing great trouble in this respect, especially in the handling of the films, which were crude, both in the supporting stock and everything else.*

America's First Movie Theater

William Reed (right) was one of six original motion picture machine operators. At the time, Reed was in charge of Edison's Kinetoscopes in the Boston vicinity. On June 15, 1896, less than two months after the original exhibition of the Vitascope at Koster and Bial's, he left his position and headed south with Rock and Wainwright.

The city of New Orleans was considered the jewel of Louisiana and this is where Rock and company headed. Upon their arrival in New Orleans, the trio had to locate a suitable venue for their new venture.

During this time period, waterfront amusement parks were extremely popular attractions throughout the country. These parks offered picnic areas, swimming, gardens, boating regattas, racing, and a stage for live entertainment featuring a variety of acts.

In that mix of contemporary popular culture, these amusement resorts offered the perfect venue for moving picture exhibitions. In addition, most amusement parks were located on streetcar/trolley/railroad lines which

America's First Movie Theater

provided the electricity needed to operate the cameras.

Fortunately for Rock & Wainwright, New Orleans offered several waterfront options for their consideration on the shores of Lake Pontchartrain.

Lake Pontchartrain, which forms the northern border of New Orleans, is actually a brackish estuary which covers an area of 630 square miles. It was named for Louis Phélypeaux, comte de Pontchartrain from Pontchartrain City. He was the French Minister of the Marine, Chancellor, and Controller-General of Finances during the reign of France's "Sun King," Louis XIV, for whom the colony of La Louisiane was named.

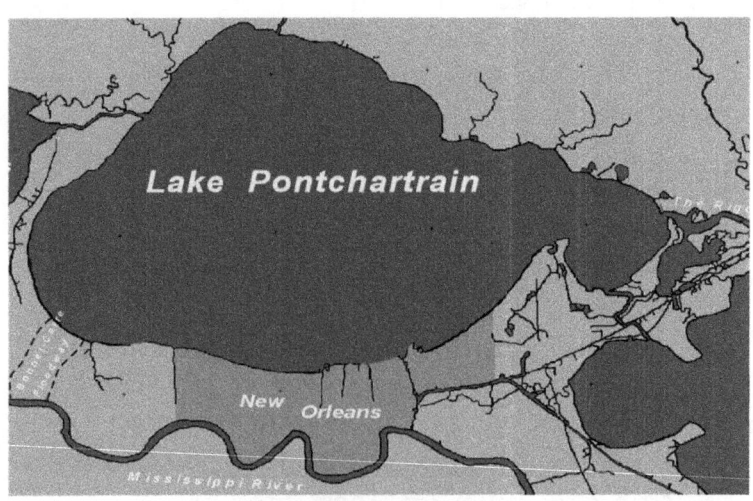

America's First Movie Theater

At the beginning of the 19th century, the New Orleans shore of the lake was mostly swamp, dotted with several communities that were mainly built over water. By the 1830's, new transportation avenues were created. Railroad tracks were extended from the city to the lake to bring boat cargo to the city from Lake Pontchartrain instead of up the Mississippi River. In addition, a new canal opened up a direct water route to the lakeshore.

These new travel options resulted in the creation of three resorts along Lake Pontchartrain enjoyed by locals and tourists: Spanish Fort; Milneburg; and New Lake End (later West End Park). Below is an ad for excursions to these parks appearing in the *Daily Picayune*:

EXCURSIONS.
FOURTH - OF - JULY.
STEAMER NEW CAMELIA.

Will make two excursions to MANDEVILLE, leaving MILNEBURG on the arrival of the 8 a. m. and 4 p. m. trains from the ELYSIAN FIELDS STREET DEPOT. RETURNING, leaves MANDEVILLE at 1 p. m. and 7:30 p. m., affording excursionists a cool and delightful trip on salt water, and a view of the FIREWORKS from the lake at WEST END, SPANISH FORT and MILNEBURG.
FARE (Round Trip) - - - - - - 50 CENTS.
Jy2—3t

America's First Movie Theater

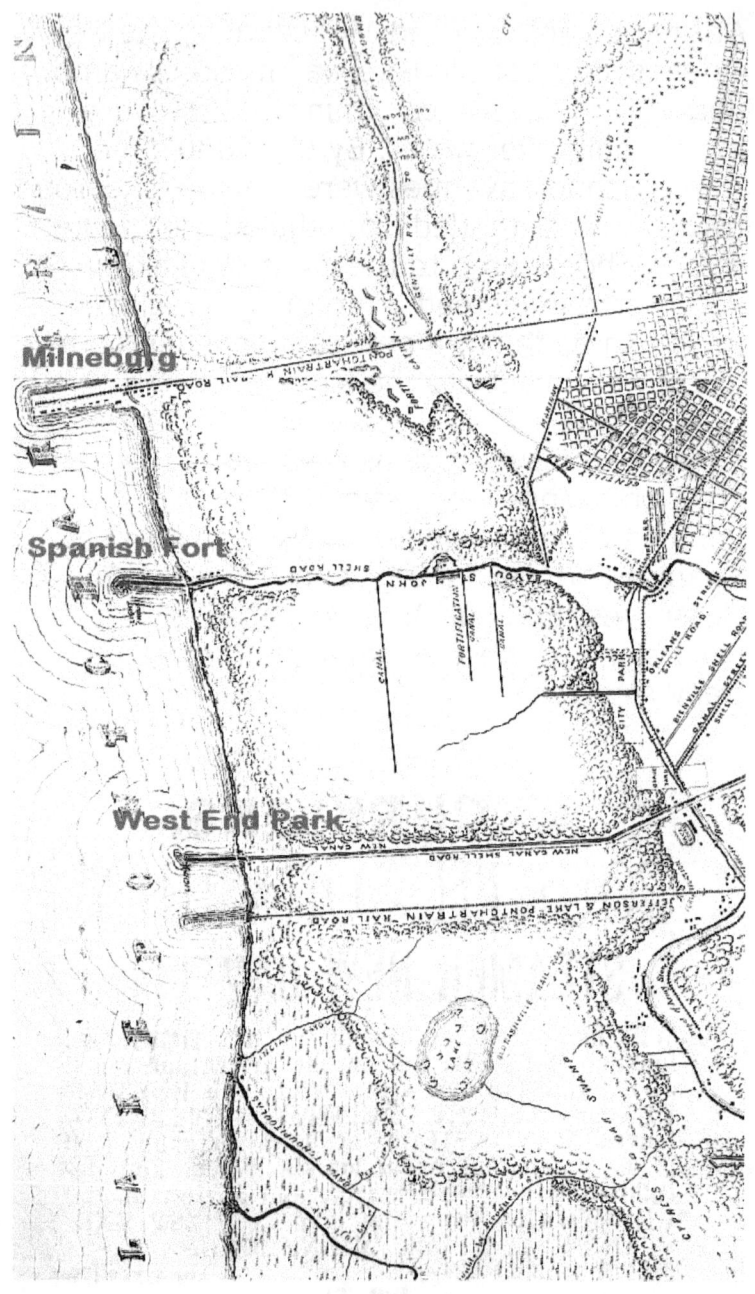

Spanish Fort

Originally an active military fort built in 1779 to protect the city from invasion via the lake, this area later became an entertainment district filled with amusement parks, restaurants, camps, and jazz.

In 1803, the fort passed to the United States under the Treaty of Cession as a military reservation. In 1823, Harvey Elkins purchased the Spanish Fort site through a special act of Congress. He built the Spanish Fort Hotel which operated from 1823-1878 (below). Within two years, he continued to build on the site, thus beginning Spanish Fort's century-long reputation as a popular resort.

America's First Movie Theater

Ownership of the property passed from Elkins to John Slidell and then to the New Orleans City and Lake Railroad.

In 1877, it was sold to Moses Schwartz, who added, over time, an amusement park, a casino, a theatre, a dancing pavilion, cabarets and several fine restaurants.

These attracted well-known entertainers, orchestras and opera companies, as well as, many noteworthy guests from all over the country. Here's an ad that appeared in the *Daily Picayune*:

GRAND CONCERT NIGHTLY
—AT—
SPANISH FORT
—BY—
Spanish Fort Band.

CHANGE PROGRAMME NIGHTLY.
TRAINS AT SHORT INTERVALS.
my30—tf

Before long, Spanish Fort became known as the "Coney Island of the South."

CONCERT HALL & GARDEN, SPANISH FORT

Among the restaurants were Over the Rhine and Tranchina's Restaurant, and the cabarets were Tokyo Gardens and The Frolics.

Milneburg

Milneburg was named for Scottish-born Alexander Milne, who developed the land in that area. In 1830, he had encouraged a group of businessmen to form the Pontchartrain Rail-Road Company,

The Pontchartrain Rail-Road was one of the first lines completed in the United States. It first opened in 1831 and operated

America's First Movie Theater

uninterrupted for over 100 years. It ran the five-mile length of Elysian Fields Avenue, running from the river in the Marigny to Lake Pontchartrain in Milneburg.

Initially, railroad service was only available by horse-drawn omni-buses, until the first steam engine arrived in 1832. The infamous, sooty exhaust of the steam engine running this line inspired the name "Smoky Mary" (below).

The railroad helped promote the early growth of Milneburg, which evolved from an industrial port to a popular resort. A long pier was built into the shallows of the lake, with a portion of the rail line running atop it, enabling ocean-going ships to dock at Milneburg.

The port boomed, and hotels, saloons, bath houses, and resorts were built around it,

America's First Movie Theater

mostly atop high wooden piers in the shallows of the lake, connected by a network of pier-like wooden boardwalks.

A series of "camps" (houses on piers in the shallows of the lake) were regularly rented out for parties, with fishing, picnics, and dancing to live bands.

One of the hotels, The Washington Hotel, became a popular stopping point for travelers while the well-to-do of New Orleans spent pleasant weekends there.

West End Park

In 1830, American businessmen in New Orleans decided to build a shipping channel from Lake Pontchartrain to the American sector of the city to compete with the established Carondelet Canal in the French section.

The arduous task of digging the canal through alligator and snake-infested swamps began in 1832. In that same year, a cholera epidemic hit the city and 6,000 people died in 20 days, many of whom were Irish.

When the canal opened for traffic, there were 8,000 Irish laborers who would never see their homes again, having succumbed to cholera and yellow fever. It was the worst single disaster to befall the Irish in their entire history in New Orleans.

Wooden jetties were constructed along the course of the canal at the lake end and soil was dredged to create a man-made land mass near the entrance to the Basin.

America's First Movie Theater

The canal (above) served as a transportation route between downtown New Orleans and Lake Pontchartrain. It also contributed to the development of a new resort area on the lake known as New Lake End.

With the canal completed, pleasure seekers could take a mule-drawn barge, complete with musical entertainment, along the New Basin Canal to New Lake End.

The United States Lighthouse Service constructed a lighthouse at the mouth the "New Canal" (next page)

America's First Movie Theater

A shell road was built along the city side of the New Basin Canal allowing carriages and streetcars to transport visitors to West End Park. In 1869, the New Orleans and Metairie Railroad Company extended its Canal Street track from the cemeteries to West End.

In 1880, the name was changed to West End Park. Before long, a bustling marine resort existed, complete with a hotel, pavilion, restaurants, bathhouses and amusement park structures, as well as large over-the-water platform.

Having its own electrical generator, the park had arc lighting before the innovation was introduced to Canal Street.

America's First Movie Theater

West End Hotel

Mannessier's Pavilion

America's First Movie Theater

Opera House

Mark Twain recounted his 1883 visit to West End ... *along a raised shell road, with a canal on one hand and a dense wood on the other.*" He described West End as a "*collection of hotels of the usual light summer-resort pattern, with broad verandas all around, and the waves of the wide and blue Lake Pontchartrain lapping the thresholds.*"

He added that the "*thousands of people come by rail and carriage to West End and to Spanish Fort every evening, and dine, listen to the bands, take strolls in the open air under the electric lights, go sailing on the lake, and entertain themselves in various and sundry other ways.*"

America's First Movie Theater

Footbridge to West End Park

America's First Movie Theater

WEST END.

1883.... ......SEASON OF............1883

Commencing May 1883.

Evening Concerts

— BY THE —

WEST END BAND,

Under the Leadership of the Accomplished Home Musician,

Prof. G. D'Aquin.

Special Engagement of the World-Renowned Cornet Virtuoso,

SIGNOR A. LIBERATI,

Commencing May 15 and Continuing for Two Weeks.

Schedule for West End Trains:

The trains of the City Railroad Company will leave as follows for West End:

DAILY.

FROM THE CITY.	FROM WEST END.
7............ A. M.	8............ A. M.
8............ A. M.	9............ A. M.
9............ A. M.	10............ A. M.
10............ A. M.	11............ A. M.
11............ A. M.	12............ M.
12............ M.	1............ P. M.
1............ P. M.	2............ P. M.
2............ P. M.	3:15............ P. M.
3............ P. M.	3:45............ P. M.

And every twenty minutes thereafter until

MOVING PICTURES MAKE THEIR LOUISIANA DEBUT

After reviewing the three available parks, Rock & Wainwright entered into a four-week contract with West End Park.

In an interview appearing in *Moving Picture World*, 1916, Rock described his adventure after securing the Louisiana territory rights for the Vitascope.

> *I took my machine and started for New Orleans. We had the May Irwin Kiss, and a lot of scenic stuff; the McKinley picture. Bill Reed was my operator. I made a contract with the West End Park for four weeks and we packed them in, renewing my contract and continuing to play the West End for several seasons.*

The next step was to find an electrical engineer to connect the Vitascope to available power lines. They hired Allen B. Blakemore, an electrical engineer from the New Orleans City and Lake Railroad.

America's First Movie Theater

In an interview appearing in the *Times Picayune*, Blakemore describes his experience with the Vitascope exhibit:

> Riding out to West End on the trolley was a wonderful way to spend a Sunday afternoon. The company I worked for lined up band concerts, vaudeville acts and prominent stage personalities to appear at West End, to get customers to ride the trolley out there.

West End Streetcar Leaving Canal St.

There were all sorts of attractions at West End. A maze of high hedges, fine restaurants and a big bandstand were built on a wood platform that extended out over the water. Before band concerts, the platform and stand were used for

America's First Movie Theater

dances and fireworks displays and then came the Vitascope. (ad from *Daily Picayune* below)

AMUSEMENTS.

GRAND CONCERT NIGHTLY
—AT—
WEST END,
—BY—
PAOLETTI'S CONCERT BAND.

OPENING SUNDAY, JUNE 28,

Edison's Wonderful Vitascope.

Je21—tf

On June 28, 1896, the first moving picture was shown at West End Park. The screening, hosted in celebration of the upcoming Fourth of July holiday, attracted thousands of area residents.

To light the projector, Blakemore, who previously had helped design the trolley system over the West End tracks and had run railroad electric current across the basin to light up the amusement platform's long string of bulbs, decided to use current from the trolley line.

America's First Movie Theater

The projector was mounted inside a small square booth with a floor six feet above ground. It was on wheels so it could be rolled backwards and forwards to get the proper picture focus. The screen was stretched across the posts in front of the bandstand.

Blakemore had to tone down the 500-volt power of the trolley line, which would be too strong for the projector. He installed a makeshift water rheostat, running the current through a barrel of water under the booth.

The New Orleans City and Lake Railway offered patrons reserved bench seating at West End for riding their car to the park. Tickets were sold in "Starter Houses" located in the neutral ground of Canal Street. (left side in the image below)

America's First Movie Theater

The following day, a review of the night's performance was printed in the *Daily Picayune*.

Edison's Vitascope at West End.

A large crowd gathered at West end last night to witness the inaugural exhibition in this city of Edison's vitascope.

A good deal of curiosity was expressed when it was first announced that the traction company was arranging to have the vitascope brought out to the resort. That sentiment seems not to have suffered during the interval which intervened between the announcement and the arrival of the apparatus. It has been arranged in a small box-house, mounted on posts, in the middle of the platform at West End, directly in front of the music stand. A screen 7x10 feet in size is placed on the music stand during the exhibition of the vitascope. It is on this screen that the pictures appear.

There were two exhibitions last night, one at 8 and one at 10 o'clock. The same pictures were shown at both. The subjects represented were Cissy Fitzgerald's skirt dance, the interior of a smithy, John Drew and May Irving

America's First Movie Theater

"doing" a kiss, a scene on a New York city elevated road, and a view of the surf breaking against the sea wall at Dover, England.

Cissy's was the only colored picture in the lot, and, therefore, was the most real; but the kiss picture pleased the audience the most, and they gave it three or four encores. The way that Drew goes through the premonitory symptoms and then squares off for action, and finally precipitates himself full upon Miss Irving's lips, are all shown with startling realism. The smith scene represented two men welding iron at an anvil, another operating the "bellows" and a fourth stacking away the finished wheels. The illusion was rendered very nearly perfect by the imitation of one of Paolotti's musicians of a clinking of hammers on the iron.

The railroad scene showed a train coming from the spectator's right, the puffing of steam, smoke, etc., all being very realistically presented. The surf picture was exquisite, the bustling of the waves being reproduced in a most natural manner. Something or other caused a good deal of vibration in the apparatus, which was repeated in the

America's First Movie Theater

picture on an exaggerated scale and interfered a little with one's appreciation of the waterscape. The performance consumed about twenty minutes, and was very much enjoyed.

The mechanism by which these pictures are produced, so as to exhibit all the various movements of life, is very simple. It consists of a small lens, such as is used in an ordinary camera. This is the vitascope proper. This lens is nearest the screen. Right behind it is a metal frame about 1-1/2 inches square, over which the picture to be reproduced passes. Behind this is a very concave-convex lense, placed directly in front of an arc light of 2000 candle-power. The principle with which the apparatus works is partly that of the kinetoscope and partly of a magic lantern. The pictures to be reproduced are photographed on kinetoscope films, each picture being an inch square. A film is about fifty feet long, and contains about 2700 separate photographs.

The film passes over a series of wheels propelled by electricity, and as the pictures are successively and at a very rapid rate brought behind the small lens mentioned above, the light from

America's First Movie Theater

the arc lamp, passing through and being focused by larger lens, projects the picture through the small lens upon the screen, magnified 600 times. Thus the automated pictures of the kinetoscope are reproduced life-size and with astonishing detail and definiteness. The only other point to be noted is that the color pictures have to be painted by hand after the photograph has been fixed on the film.

The films can, of course, be made of any length, and it is hoped that the exhibition will shortly be improved by the introduction of films 2000 feet long. It will be possible with films of this great length to represent on the screen as a continuous moving panorama anything from a prize fight to a view of Niagara Falls. Mr. Edison, who invented the vitascope, as is well known, is very anxious now to perfect the photograph so that it can be combined with the vitascope and make it possible to put before the audience a photographic reproduction of a play or an opera, together with the music or the dialogue.

America's First Movie Theater

The performance last night was the first ever given in the open air, and was, therefore, in the nature of an experiment, which it must be a source of gratification to the managers to know was entirely successful. The vitascope will continue to be exhibit nightly for four weeks, the programme being varied weekly by the addition of new films.

Cissy Fitzgerald's Skirt Dance

Map showing the basic layout of West End Park in 1896.

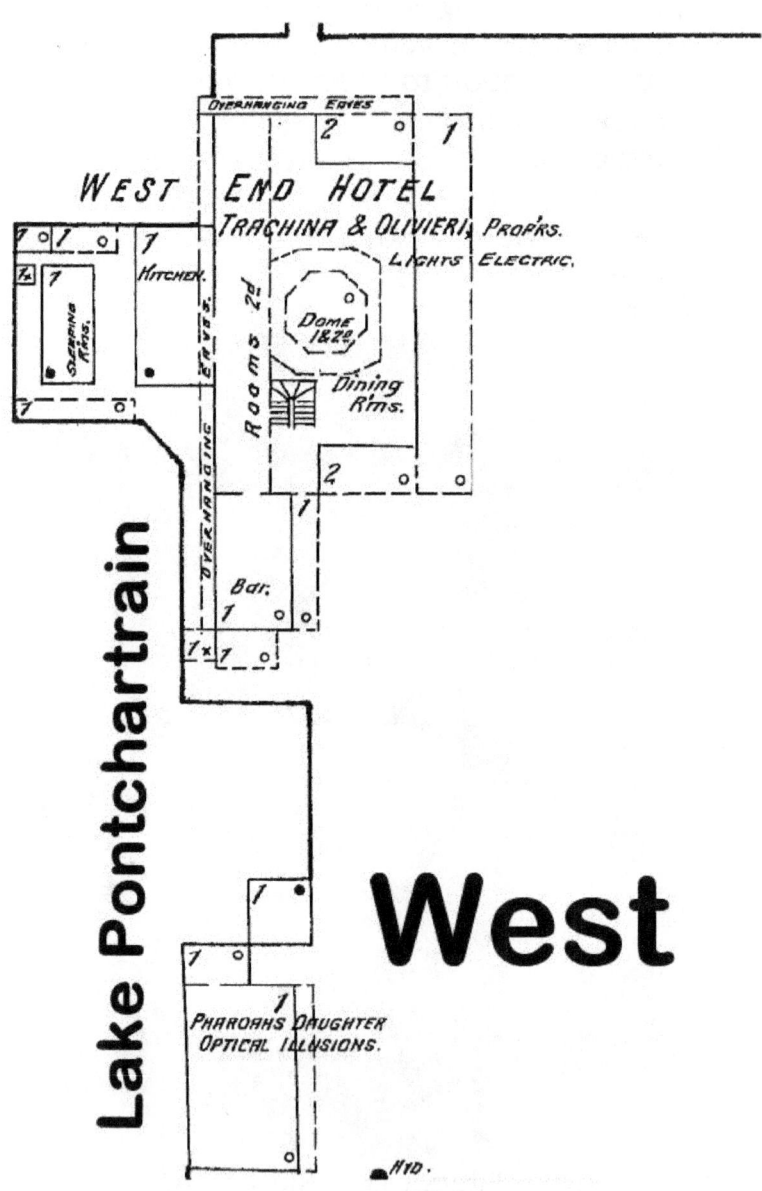

America's First Movie Theater

Map showing the basic layout of West End Park in 1896.

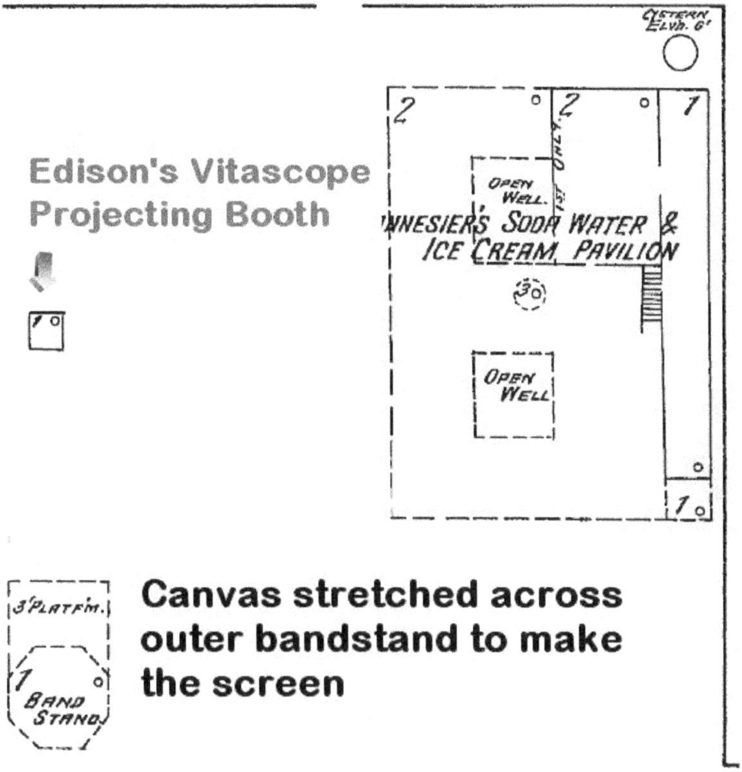

Edison's Vitascope Projecting Booth

Canvas stretched across outer bandstand to make the screen

End

America's First Movie Theater

The "*Kiss*" (below) was so controversial that it was denounced by the local clergy and caused enough publicity that Rock agreed to show it only by "special request" (which, according to Rock, was quite often).

These films were not fillers for the regular band concerts but a major part of an evening's program. The movie shows ran for the summer season.

After the four week run, Rock & Wainwright made a decision that would change their direction, and the history of the movie industry.

THE FIRST MOVIE THEATER IN AMERICA OPENS ITS DOORS

The crowds at West End Park were so enthusiastic that Rock and Wainwright decided to open a permanent home for their Vitascope. This was a very risky move.

Exhibitions of the Vitascope had been made at theaters, halls and open-air venues but only as a part of a live entertainment program. A temporary exhibit had also been build at the Cotton States Exposition in Atlanta, but it was a financial failure. There were no "permanent" facilities exclusively designed for exhibition of films only, so there was no way to determine if people would come just to see the films.

In addition, there were significant costs involved in setting up a new venue, including facility rental, seating, advertising, etc. At the time, many in the industry, including Thomas Edison, believed that the moving picture craze was merely a passing fad. Despite the looming questions, the partners began their search for the perfect location for their new venture. They recognized that a well-known

America's First Movie Theater

convenient location was essential so they began their search on Canal Street.

Canal Street

Canal Street was the retail and merchandising heart of New Orleans in 1896. Its width, measuring 171', was the result of land set aside for a canal by the federal government. The canal was supposed to connect the Mississippi River to the Basin Canal (also called the Carondelet Canal). The proposed canal was never built, but the result was a 171 foot wide commons area, which gradually evolved into a street with a neutral ground.

With the influx of Americans after the Louisiana Purchase in 1803, Canal Street became the primary separation line between Creole New Orleans downriver and the growing American sector above Canal. Cultural tension between those of European descent and the Americans tended to keep the groups within their respective neighborhoods, but Canal Street emerged as a "neutral ground" of sorts, a place where all New Orleanians came for shopping, business and transportation.

It is commonly believed that Canal Street's status as a "neutral ground" between these two sometimes hostile groups is the origin of the New Orleans term "neutral ground" referring to street medians city wide.

America's First Movie Theater

Between 1820 and 1850, the street saw a mixture of residential and commercial construction, including several major residences. In the years leading up to the Civil War, commercial building intensified, with a number of cast-iron fronted buildings constructed on both sides of the street.

As time progressed, residential uses moved further uptown, and by the outbreak of the war, Canal Street had been transformed into a vibrant commercial center. After the war, construction continued, with more ornately detailed buildings in the popular Italianate style.

In addition, Canal Street was the epicenter of the railroad and streetcars lines that served all areas of the city (below).

America's First Movie Theater

Canal Street 1857

By 1896, Canal Street's thriving commercial and amusement environment offered the ideal location for a new entertainment venue.

Vitascope Finds a Home and Makes Movie History

On July 18, 1896, Rock & Wainwright rented a storefront located at 623 Canal Street.

The original 3-story building on the corner of Canal and Exchange was built in 1832 by the Bank of New Orleans (below).

The building was purchased in 1876 by Henry Clay Warmoth. Warmoth, an Illinois native, was an attorney, Union Civil War officer, and Louisiana elected official. He served as Governor of Louisiana from 1868 to 1872.

America's First Movie Theater

Warmoth was impeached in 1872 during election contest over his successor.

In 1890, Warmoth was appointed U.S. Collector of Customs in New Orleans. Warmoth was the landlord of the building at the time Rock & Wainright entered into the rental agreement for the property.

With the rental agreement completed, the partners fitted the storefront as a showroom with 400 chairs and a projection room. Large sheets of black canvas covered the windows to keep out the penetrating sunlight. A white fabric was stretched across a frame mounted at the front of the room.

Without much fanfare, Vitascope Hall opened to the public on Sunday, July 26, 1896 – becoming the first seated indoor theater in the United States (next page),

Each session ran for twenty minutes with a ten minute break in between each session. The first session started at 10:00 a.m. and these sessions ran until 5:00 p.m.; night sessions varied from 6:00 to 10:00 p.m. and 7:00 till 11:00 p.m. Admission price was 10 cents. For an additional 10 cents, patrons could view the projector and for another dime take home a piece of the film clippings from the floor.

America's First Movie Theater

In an interview appearing in *Moving Picture World* dated August 13, 1921, projectionist Billy Reed said that so many patrons demanded to be allowed to inspect the projector that they finally charged fifty cents

America's First Movie Theater

for a visit to the projection room, which was indeed a "booth" and nothing more. They also sold film clippings for ten cents apiece or three for twenty-five cents. They went like hot cakes and the revenue from visits to the projection room were considerable.

The following announcement ad appeared in the *Daily Picayune*:

Vitascope Hall,
623 CANAL STREET.

THE VITASCOPE

Is no longer at the WEST END, but is now at the above, where daily exhibitions will be given, with an entirely new series of pictures.

See Niagara Falls.
COMMENCING TO-DAY.

From 10 a. m. till 6 p. m. and from 7 p. m. till 11 p. m.

Admission - - - - - 10c.

For the next nine weeks, Vitascope Hall opened to packed crowds. Their programs changed regularly. Here are a series of advertisements appearing in the *Daily Picayune*:

America's First Movie Theater

Vitascope Hall,

623 CANAL ST. AND EXCHANGE PLACE.

THE GREAT CRAZE OF THE DAY,

EDISON'S VITASCOPE.

New series of thrilling views. Photographic motion at last perfected. The dream of a century realized. The whole town startled and Vitascope Hall crowded to the doors by brilliant audiences, day and night.

ADMISSION, 10 CENTS.

WAINWRIGHT & ROCK,
SOLE OWNERS AND MANAGERS.

Southern states and territory rights for sale.

au2—tf

VITASCOPE HALL.
623 Canal, Cor. Exchange Place.
THE CENTURY'S MARVEL.
Edison Vitascope.

Pronounced by the entire press to be the town's reigning "fad" in summer theatricals. Scientists amazed and the public charmed by this greatest and most effective of all stage inventions.

ADMISSION......10c.

Exhibitions from 10 a. m. to 8 p. m., and from 9 p. m. to 10 p. m.

Entire change of programme morning and evening.

WAINWRIGHT & ROCK,
Sole Owners and Managers.

Southern state and territory rights for sale.

America's First Movie Theater

> **VITASCOPE HALL,**
> 623 Canal, Corner Exchange Place.
> THE SCIENTISTS' CRAZE,
> EDISON'S VITASCOPE.
> Fourth week and continued triumph of the marvelous motion pictures. The talk of two continents, and the delight of countless multitudes. More new views this week. See
> LUCILLE STINGIS,
> the pretty dancer, New York's latest and greatest success, to-day at the VITASCOPE.
> ADMISSION, 10 CENTS.
> Doors open from 10 a. m. to 3 p. m., and from 6 p. m. to 10 p. m.
> WAINWRIGHT & ROCK,
> SOLE OWNERS AND MANAGERS.
> Southern State and Territory Rights for sale.
> au23--tf

Contrary to popular belief, clipping coupons is not an activity of the 20th century. Vitascope Hall, in conjunction with the *Daily Picayune*, offered a coupon for free admittance to the Hall's daily programs:

> **The Picayune's Vitascope Coupon.**
> **WEDNESDAY, SEPTEMBER 23.**
> This coupon admits on the day of its date any child under the age of ten years (accompanied by an adult) to the VITASCOPE.
> au29--tf*   WAINWRIGHT & ROCK.

Rock and Wainwright cleared over $4,000 for the season. They were the only ones out of about forty buyers of states rights on the

America's First Movie Theater

Vitascope who came out ahead financially; all the rest went broke on the deal.

Rock attributed their success to the fact that he knew considerable about electricity and Reed knew how to handle the film and projection.

Entertainment programs at this time period were based on seasons. At the end of the 1896 season, the partners closed the doors planning to return for the next season with new films, which were scarce in those days.

VITASCOPE HALL.

LAST DAYS

OF THE PRESENT SUCCESSFUL SEASON.

THE VITASCOPE,

WITH ALL NEW VIEWS,

Ending Wednesday Sept. 30.

WAINWRIGHT & ROCK,

SOLE OWNERS AND MANAGERS.

s27—4t

Rock and Wainwright Return to New Orleans the Next Season

By the time the partners returned in March of 1897, other venues were available for the Vitascope. In addition to returning to West End Park, they also exhibited at other theaters such as Grunewald's and the Grand Opera House.

Rock and Wainwright would return again to West End Park as well as other theaters in the area for the summer season in 1898. After that season, Rock moved back home to New York and began a partnership with J. Stuart Blackton and Albert E. Smith. By 1907, this partnership resulted in the creation of the Vitagraph Company, the most prolific American film production company, producing many famous silent films. Vitagraph was bought by Warner Bros. in 1925.

There is some question as to what happened to Wainright. Some sources report that he went to Europe to help acquire films for Vitagraph. Other indications are that he returned to the carnival.

William Reed continued as projectionist for a number of companies, retiring as one of the most respected projectionists in American history.

EPILOGUE

In 1911, *New Orleans Times-Democrat* reporter Flo Field lamented the fact that after fifteen years, the accomplishments of Messrs. Rock, Wainwright and Reed were long forgotten, even though the movie industry continued to grow and prosper.

Here is the article as it appeared *in Moving Picture News* citing the article which appeared in the *New Orleans Times-Democrat.*

Moving Pictures
By Flo Field

The anniversary is at hand, a few days this way or that, of the first moving picture exhibit in New Orleans. Fifteen years ago out at West End a curious, wondering, half incredulous crowd gathered to see the incredible display of living, moving pictures, produced by the fifth machine in the United States that was the product of Edison's genius.

It is an anniversary that will cause no stir; in fact, it will be scarcely remembered by even the few who worked like Trojans with the difficulty of an inadequate outfit and inefficient apparatus such as would stagger the operator of today, who has nothing to do

America's First Movie Theater

but turn a crank. By the great gaping public who looked and looked and could scarcely believe their own eyes, it has dropped into oblivion with other anniversaries of the same kind, continuing to prove what a big child that public is, forgetting constantly which its benefits began, only asking for more and newer plaything. And yet but a touch is needed to make the child remember, and remember vividly, as children do, that evening of grown-up fairy tale, which the impossible -- the thing that couldn't -- happened! the slow slipping bayou, the great, soft-shadowy lake, the mystery of swamp with its ragged, dim outline of moss-hung trees against the sapphire night sky, the old puzzle gardens and "maze" and "lover's lane," fragrant with roses and sweet olive, fall faintly on the mind's screen as a mystic frame for that sharp, dazzling square out on the great platform in which pictures came true.

Fifteen years ago! And one has seen and forgotten enough moving pictures to wrap around the equator, but the marvels of those first forty-foot films lingers yet. There was the Cissy Fitzgerald picture, that wink that was so famous, and the May Irwin kiss picture, and one can still see the more astounding view of the New York elevated Railroad and the rushing trains of a station scene. One felt, one recollects, that one was in imminent danger of being run over. The morning paper next day commented upon the "realistic manner" in which the 'steam, smoke, etc. was present!"

We do not, primarily, take our pleasures sadly in the south. We get all the magic that is in them. You will recall it was so when we finally were invaded by electric cars. We came in droves from the side streets to watch them go by; our friends, fortunate enough to live on "the avenue," held front gallery levees, sort of all-day box parties, to witness the performance of street cars flying by without apparently head nor tail to 'em! We welcomed them with a fearful enthusiasm and not a few of us also opposed them with the sneaking believe that they were "demon-haunted." The first four-horse coach in the city was a stock circus to us, and the coaching parties which the wealthy, progressive owner gave once in a while, caused about as much thrill as the passing of the band wagon, nor did we miss the band when the footman blew his fabulous trumpet. The first automobiles, the first phonographs, the first piano players, they all found us unprepared, pristine in our appreciation, unspoiled in our delight by the sophistication that robs.

America's First Movie Theater

The moving picture descended upon us as the spangled parachute jumper did upon old Uncle Ebeon in the cornfield. As the one seemed heaven-sent, so the picture appeared to us nothing if not actual. Why, some of us thought they were sure enough people! and when a stunt was finished we often caught ourselves applauding the performer.

One remembers, in particular, one picture of a beautiful lady acrobat, who was shown in a trapeze act, and as she suspended herself by one hand and straightened her body out at right angles Jim, who was one's best beau at the time and keen on sports and appreciative to the last degree, burst into tumultuous clapping and was so revealed to the breathless audience as the lights went up. As the crowd realized Jim's naiveté and its own narrow escape, it gave vent to a great crowd laugh and bent its good-natured banter upon Jim's chagrin and one's flaming mortification. It all seemed reason enough then for a stormy parting.

It was, as has been said, a primitive equipment as compared with the outfits of to-day. The machine itself weighed between 250 and 300 pounds, where as now the weight is scarcely over 75 pounds. It was of the spool bank type, run by a one-eighth horse power motor, and, considering

America's First Movie Theater

the skill and general experience required, it is not surprising that the operators commanded salaries of $50 and $75 a week. In the little white room which was the operator's box at West End was "Bill Reed," one of the oldest, ablest operators in the picture business and to whom we promptly gave the picturesque title of "Sir William Vitagraph." That hat box in which he worked possessed fascinations. We regarded it as something between a jewel casket and a jack-in-the-box. We applied, five hundred a night, to get inside and see what happened. Sometimes he let a celebrity up. Lesser applicants never knew what was seen; all that the celebrity ever explained was that it was the hottest place he'd ever been in or hoped to be in! And in a temperature that so beggared description the operator looked after electricity, motor and film. Off in an outbuilding, on his knees, another enthusiast in the business pumped away at the gasoline engine that supplied power to the operator. The pictures lasted twenty minutes. Crowds of 12,000 and more flocked out on the old dummy trains, trooped over the slow, slipping bayou to sit spellbound for those twenty magic minutes, and wotted nothing that it was so prosaically accomplished, one man on his knees pumping a motor, the other in a dripping shirt manipulating the awkward possibilities of light and film of a

America's First Movie Theater

machine that had no shutter between the film and the lens.

But now the wonder is worn away, and with the wonder the happy curiosity over the cause. We accept anything on the moving picture screen and not only never give even an idle thought to the operator's box and its mysteries, but look upon the most thrilling play, the most dangerous situation and wonderful scenery, and never ask how it is all done. Fifteen years ago, when we were in such excitement over forty-foot films, the newspapers prophesied that they would reach a length of 2,000 feet. The reproduction of the Passion Play requires a 5,000-foot film, and the improvements that have taken place in this span of time are on the same scale of comparisons. New Orleans was the first city in the world to have a ten-cent moving picture show, the "Vitascope," as it was called, at 623 Canal Street. Now every small town in the Union that has electric lights has a picture house. There are about 600 moving picture houses in New York; Los Angeles has more; Chicago has over a thousand, and the manufacturers in the business are too numerous to mention. The business as a whole has reached almost immeasurable proportions. the large picture companies have the most magnificent studios and their own stock companies constantly in

America's First Movie Theater

rehearsal and acting before the camera. In the production of a picture no expense is spared. Recently to perform a picture play, "The Trapper's Daughter," the Vitagraph Company sent their stock company of actors to Alaska to get the proper setting. Another company, the Kalem Company, has just sent a troop to Ireland for the real scenic background.

As you can tell, Ms. Field was very upset that after fifteen years, the details and events of how the first movie theater came about were already forgotten.

What would Ms. Field think to learn that 120 years have now passed, and this oversight has not yet been corrected.

REFERENCES

BOOKS

Ceram, C. W., *Archaeology of the Cinema*. London, England, Thames and Hudson London, 1965

Cook, Olive, *Movement in Two Dimensions*. London, England, Anchor Press, 1963

Musser, Charles, *The Emergence of Cinema; The American Screen to 1907, Volume 1*. New York, NY, Maxwell Macmillan International, 1990

Poole, E. and S. Poole. *Louisiana Film History: A Comprehensive Overview Beginning 1896*. Donaldsonville, LA: Margaret Media, Inc., 2012

Poole, E. and S. Poole. *Hollywood on the Bayou*. Gretna, LA: Learn About Network, L.L.C, 2011

Poole, E. and S. Poole. *Learn About Movie Posters*. Chattanooga, TN: Iguide Media, Inc., 2002

Ramsaye, Terry, *A Million and One Nights, A History of the Motion Picture*. London, England, Frank Cass & Co., Ltd., 1954

Robertson, Patrick, *Guinness Book of Movie Facts & Feats*. Middlesex, England, Guinness Publishing Ltd., 1993

Toulet, Emmanuelle, *Birth of the Motion Picture*. New York, NY, Harry N. Abrams, Inc., 1995

LEGAL CITATIONS

New Orleans C. & L. R. Co. v. New Orleans, 143 U.S. 192 (1892)

NEWSPAPERS & MAGAZINES

Daily Picayune
Moving Picture World

Motion Picture News

Journal of the Society of Motion Picture Engineers

WEBSITES

Hollywood on the Bayou - www.hollywoodonthebayou.com

Louisiana Digital Library - www.louisdl.louislibraries.org/

LA Library Connection - http://lalibcon.state.lib.la.us

National Park Services - www.nps.gov

America's First Movie Theater

INDEX

Accordion Player, 29
American Mutoscope Company, 28, 40, 41
Aristotle, 5
Armat, Thomas, 43, 47, 48, 50, 52, 54
Babbage, Charles 9
Bacon, Friar Roger, 9
Baltimore Sun, 52
Bank of New Orleans, 97
Biograph, 40
Blakemore, Allen B., 81-84
Canal Street, 76, 84, 94-97
chronophotography, 23, 24
Cinematographe, 35- 37
cinematography, 3, 28
Cotton States and Int'l Expos, 47, 50- 53, 93
Daedelum, 13
Daily Picayune Ads, 67, 70, 80, 83, 100-102,
Daily Picayune, 85-89
daVinci, Leonardo, 5
Dickson, William Kennedy Laurie, 30, 40
Eastman, George, 30
Edison, Thomas, 27- 29, 32-34, 37-38, 40, 42,
  47-48, 52, 55- 57, 59- 61, 65, 85, 93, 105
Eidoloscope, 39, 53
Elkins, Harvey, 69-70
Fantoscope, 11
Field, Flo, 105-111
Fitzgerald, Cissy, 85, 89, 106
Frolics, The, 71
Gammon, Frank R., 42
Gilmore, W. E., 38, 40

Goodwin, Hannibal W., 30
Harrison, Frank, 53
Herschel, John, 9
Holland Brothers, 33
Horner, William George, 13, 19
Horse in Motion, The, 16, 17
Huygens, Christian, 5
Janssen, Pierre Jules Cesar, 23
Jenkins, Charles Francis, 43-48, 50, 52
Journal of the Society of Motion Picture Engineers, 47
Kinetoscope, 30- 34, 37-38, 40, 42, 47, 53, 59, 65, 87, 88
KMCD, 40
Koster and Bials, 56- 59, 65,
Lake Pontchartrain, 66, 74-75
Latham Loop, 40, 54
Latham, Grey, 38, 53
Latham, Otway, 38
Lauste, Eugene, 38, 40
Le Prince, Adolphe, 28
Le Prince, Elizabeth, 28
Le Prince, Louis Aime Augustin, 24-29
Leeds Bridge, 27-28
Lumiere Brothers, 27, 34, 37-38
Lumiere, Auguste, 34
Lumiere, Louis 34
magic lantern, 5-8
Mannessier's Pavilion, 77
Marey, Etienne-Jules, 23
Mark Twain, 78
May Irwin Kiss, 81, 86, 90
Milne, Alexander, 71

Milneburg, 67-68, 71-74
Moving Picture World, 63, 81, 99, 105-111
Mutoscope, 41
Muybridge, Eadweard, 16, 18, 23-24, 30
New Canal Lighthouse, 75
New Lake End, 67, 75
New Orleans and Metairie Railroad Co., 76
New Orleans City and Lake Railroad, 81, 84
New Orleans Times Democrat, 105-111
Niepce, Joseph, 7
Opera House, 78
optical toys, 9, 11
Over the Rhine, 71
Paris, John Ayrton, 9
Pauvre Pierrot, 22
persistence of vision, 3-4, 11
Phantasmascope, 11
Phantoscope, 42-44, 48-49, 53-55
Phenakistoscope, 9, 11-13, 19
phi phenomenon, 3-4
phonograph cylinder, 29
Plateau, Joseph, 11, 19
Pontchartrain Rail-Road, 71
Praxinoscope, 20-21
Raff and Gammon, 48, 53, 55, 60-61, 63
Raff, Norman C., 42
Reed, William, 65, 81, 104
Reeves, Richard, 5
Reynaud, Charles Emile, 19, 21-22
Richmond Telegram, 44, 55
Rock and Wainwright, 64, 66, 81, 90, 93, 97, 103,-104
Rock, William T. "Pop," 62- 65, 81, 104

Roget, Peter Mark, 3
Roundhay Garden scene, 27-28
Schwartz, Moses, 69
Slidell, John, 70
Smoky Mary, 72
Solomon, 5
Spanish Fort Hotel, 69
Spanish Fort, 67-71, 78
Stanford, Leland, 16, 18
starter houses, 84
Talbot, Henry Fox, 8
Thaumatrope, 9, 10
Theatre Optique, 21, 22
Tokyo Gardens, 71
Tranchina's Restaurant, 71
Transactions of the Society of Motion Picture Engineers, 44
View from a Window at Le Gras, 8
Vitagraph Company, 104
Vitascope Hall, 98-104, 110
Vitascope, 54-59, 61, 63-65, 81-83, 85, 87-89, 93, 104, 110
Wainwright, Walter, 62, 64, 81, 104
Walgensten, Thomas Rasumussen, 5
Warmoth, Henry Clay, 97-98
Wertheimer, Max, 3
West End Hotel, 77
West end Park, 67-68, 74-93, 104-105
Zoetrope, 9, 13, 14, 19, 20
Zoogyroscope, 18
Zoopraxiscope, 18. 30

www.ingramcontent.com/pod-product-compliance
Lightning Source LLC
Chambersburg PA
CBHW071705040426
42446CB00011B/1927